Do Your Own
UPHOLSTERY

DO YOUR OWN
UPHOLSTERY

by Rena Cross

W. Foulsham & Co. Ltd., London

New York   Toronto   Capetown   Sydney

W. FOULSHAM & CO. LTD.
Yeovil Road, Slough, Berks. England.

ISBN 0–572–00845–7

Designed by Loraine Dixon

Photoset, printed and bound
in Great Britain by
Redwood Burn Limited
Trowbridge & Esher

Contents

Introduction

Upholstery is always far easier to do than to read about . . . or to write about, for that matter. Anyone can reupholster a chair in some sort of fashion, and many of us start our early upholstery efforts with a minimum of foreknowledge. There are certain techniques which make our work easier, and the results neater and more long-lasting, and it is with these techniques that this book deals in principle, with particular emphasis on the appearance of the finished product. A good armchair is with us for a long, long time.

Increasingly these days, home upholstery is becoming a required personal skill, since the cost of a good-looking comfortable new armchair is very high. Professional upholsterers are expensive and many of them have bookings for a year ahead.

The completion of the exercises in the first two chapters will save you more than £40, and this represents pretty good value.

Can anyone learn to upholster? Yes, anyone who can sew a seam, hammer in a tack, measure a straight line and read directions.

This book is not intended as light bedside reading. When you read it, do so with the appropriate article of furniture in front of you, so that directions which may seem a little obscure in print become clear. By running a finger over the correct seam, reminding yourself by glancing at, for instance, the 'top of the inside back', or realising what is meant by such terms as 'a wing and arm in one piece', will help you to understand the instructions more easily.

Since the resurgence of interest in home upholstery, it has become easier to buy the necessary materials and implements, and many department stores carry them in their craft sections. Or your local dealer in antique furniture, if he does his own upholstering, may well divulge his own sources of supply. Where suppliers are not particularly plentiful, enquiries should be made to dealers in handicraft materials, such as Dryad of Leicester.

Chapter One

Basic Arm Chair Repairs

The most common problem in upholstery is undoubtedly that of the aged but not necessarily antique armchair. Once handsome and comfortable, it now presents an appearance of extreme shabbiness and lumpiness, and its broken springs obtrude into the tender parts of one's anatomy. Only the high cost of a replacement (which may parallel its shape very closely, because chair fashions have 'come round' again) prevents us from tipping the dustman to take it away.

In its day, of course, it was probably a very good chair, built by a craftsman, and designed to stand up to considerable ill-usage. It would have lasted considerably longer, if a few running repairs had been undertaken as they became necessary, but an armchair is a curiously neglected article of furniture where maintenance is concerned, and when it starts to run down it quickly comes to ruin.

Let us consider such a chair, and as we look into its internal structure we may well find that there is less to do than we thought. No process in upholstery is difficult, although there are certain techniques which should be learnt, and this is what this book is all about.

When dealing with ancient furniture, the best place to work, weather permitting, is in the garden, or garage because you will probably get a considerable amount of stuffing out of your chair, much of it fragmented with wear and time. The worst place to work is on the living-room carpet, unless you cover it completely with newspaper, because the removal of fragmented hair or fibre is, to say the least, messy. If you have tiles or lino in the kitchen, the floor can more easily be swept up afterwards, but unless you intend to finish in one day, which is heavy going for a beginner, you will either have to work round it until it is finished, or carry it back and forth if your kitchen is small, and you want to cook a meal. This rather dampening advice is simply designed to avoid the development of a dislike of upholstery engendered by the continued presence of a large disembowelled chair just where you find it most inconvenient.

Turn your chair upside down, and you will almost certainly find a piece of hessian or calico tacked to the bottom of the seat. This is called the *base cover*, and if it is in good condition, you can wash it and use it again. It will almost certainly have stretched, so that when you tack it down again (your last operation in the exercise) you will be tacking along a new line, and it won't matter if the old tack line is a bit torn. On the other hand, you may consider this parsimonious, as the material for a new base cover only costs a few pence.

Removing Tacks

To remove your base cover, you are going to have to take the tacks out, and this is best done with a *ripping chisel*, if you have one, but if you don't, you can use an ordinary chisel, and a wooden mallet rather than an ordinary hammer, which might damage the chisel head. Failing a wooden mallet, you can wrap the head of a hammer in cloth, binding it with thread, or borrow a panel-beater's hammer.

(You will notice that throughout this book, expenses are kept to a minimum. It always seems a poor policy to advise expensive equipment for a new project, where cheaper substitutes are available, because it introduces a compulsive feeling that the project must be completed to justify the expense. Projects should be completed because we want to complete them, and for no other reason.)

A ripping chisel simply rips the tacks out cleanly, but if you use an ordinary chisel and mallet or hammer, hold the chisel blade on the edge of the tack head and hit it smartly with the hammer. The opposite edge of the tack head will rise, and the tack can be pulled out with pliers. Pull the tack out *with* the grain of the wood, and not against it, to avoid splitting the wood.

You will be constantly pulling out tacks while re-upholstering, and it is as well to know the easiest and most efficient way.

An interesting George IV chair with fluted back. Besides needing a new cover, the seat has become extremely uncomfortable.

The chair, supported for easy access, showing the base cover.

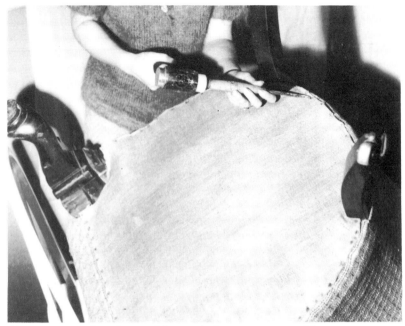

Removing tacks. A panel beater's hammer is used here to prevent damage to the chisel handle, but a mallet is more normally used.

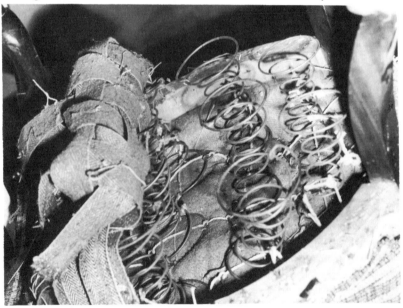

Removal of the base cover reveals webbing, which has been moved aside to show the corded springs. The webbing will be renewed, but springs and cording are in good condition.

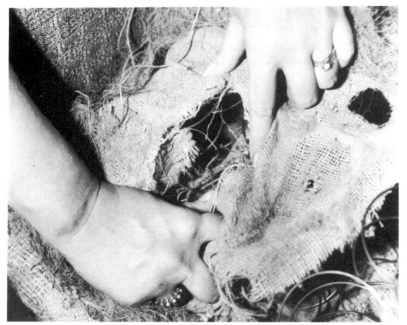

Under the seat cover. Remains of a sprung cushion incorporated into the seat at a previous reupholstering.

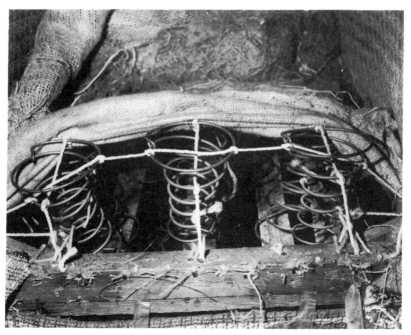

The removal of seat cover, padding and debris shows the hard edge at the front of the seat. The hessian covering has been pulled back to show the first row of corded springs.

Once you have got the base cover off, you will probably be treated to a shower of dust and crumbled fibre, and when this has died away, you will almost certainly see a number of webbing bands stretched from one side of the wooden seat frame to the other, and from back to front. You will also see strong springs rising up from this webbing. But their interest, at the moment, is purely academic, and you will be tackling them from the top. All you do at the moment is to clean the bottom of the webbing thoroughly, and turn the chair the right way up again.

New Upholstery or Old

You are going to have to remove the actual cover of the seat to effect repairs, but before you do so you are going to have to decide whether you are going to preserve your existing upholstery, albeit with a little cleaning up, or whether you are going to do a complete re-covering job.

If the present upholstery is good enough to keep, you will only have to unpick and untack enough to enable you to work easily, so that you have as little to resew or retack as possible.

In this chapter, we deal only with repairs where the original fabric is left intact, and deal with complete re-covering in the next chapter.

Repairing the Chair Seat

If there is a loose cushion, remove it.

Remove the seat cover, which will probably be tacked on all sides to the wooden frame rails. It is just possible that it may be continuous with the back cover, which must be removed for a short way, for ease of working. (Armchairs come in such variety that it is impossible to give directions for every type. Commonsense plays a great part in upholstery. Cover pieces obviously were put on when the chair was made, and therefore can be removed and replaced in the same way. If your chair does not seem to conform to a standard pattern, don't be above taking notes if you remove or displace fabric pieces. It may save you considerable trouble when it comes to replacement.)

Beneath your seat cover, you will almost certainly find a layer of wadding, and then a layer of padding, usually of rubberized hair, coconut fibre or cotton waste. If it is in reasonable condition, and not entirely frayed away, you can use it again, possibly with additional fresh stuffing of similar type. Put it on one side for the moment.

Beneath the padding, there will be another hessian cover, and beneath that a set of springs. The tops of the springs will be stitched to the hessian, and the stitches will have to be cut before the hessian can be removed.

You will see that the base of the springs are attached to the webbing that you saw from the bottom of the chair when you removed the base cover.

When the chair was first made, the webbing was stretched tight, each spring was stitched firmly into position where two webbing pieces crossed, the springs were corded to each other, and to the framework edge, and the spring tops stitched to the hessian cover. Now, in all probability, the webbing has slackened, the springs are 'every which way', some possibly strained out of shape, some with broken cords, and it is this that causes the chair seat to become lumpy and uncomfortable.

Tightening Webbing

This is your first job in repairing your chair, and to do it properly, you really need a webbing stretcher, because the webbing is going to have to be strained really tight. Some people will tell you that you can strain webbing over a block of wood placed against the outside of the framework, but this is really only practicable when you are replacing old webbing with new, and have plenty of slack. In restretching old webbing, you gain an extra $2\frac{1}{2}$ cm. (1 in.) at the most, and need some implement that will firmly grip a short webbing end. A proper webbing stretcher is a good investment, because it enables you to do the job easily and efficiently, and will last you through a lifetime of upholstery.

If any pieces of webbing are broken or badly frayed, they will have to be replaced. (See page 39) Where they are in good condition:

(a) Remove tacks from one end of the webbing. The webbing will be folded *under* at one end, and *over* at the other, and in this case, remove tacks from the folded-over end.

(b) Catch the loose webbing end in your webbing stretcher, and stretch it downwards, over the edge of the frame. If you have a 'show wood' frame, i.e. one that is visible after the upholstery is finished, be especially careful not to bruise the wood with the stretcher. A wrapping of corrugated cardboard or rag around the frame will prevent this.

(c) Still stretching the webbing, place in one central tack to fasten the webbing to the frame, and then two more to form a triangle. (You will find the other end of the webbing tacked in similar fashion.) You may feel that you need three hands for the job, but the following tip may help you to overcome the difficulty. Before you start your stretching operations, place your three tacks in a triangle through a piece of brown paper, so that they stand upright, and can easily be knocked into place with your hammer, and the brown paper ripped away.

(d) Turn over the webbing end, and secure with two more tacks.

(e) Tighten all the webbing in one direction, and then all the webbing in the other direction. Make sure that every piece is fully stretched so that the tension is equal.

Repairing Springing

If you have damaged or broken springs, the best course is to take one to your local hardware shop for a replacement. Springs are more or less standard in size, but it is better to be sure of a perfect match. However, springs are more usually simply displaced owing to broken cording, and a broken spring is a rarity.

Restitching

With luck, the damage will be limited to a few broken ties that secure the spring bottoms to the webbing. These can be repaired by stitching them down again with strong twine and a curved upholstery needle. Springs are stitched down in three or four places where the webbing pieces cross. Tie off your stitching with a firm knot beneath the webbing.

Cording

Springs are corded together in rows, and the ends of the cords fastened to the framework. Cording keeps the springs upright, and ensures that, when sat on, they go down in unison. (It would be very uncomfortable if they didn't.)

There are a number of different types of cord which can be used, including special spring cord, or sisal or jute cord. Woven cords of the 'blind cord' type are not suitable, as they tend to stretch and fray.

Illustrations of cording always make the operation look far more difficult than it really is, and it is one of the processes easier to perform than to describe. For this reason we apologise for including rather laboured directions, but it is essential that springs should be corded correctly, or the chair seat will be very uncomfortable indeed.

Where you have a single broken cord, you will simply have to renew the cording in that row, but we are going to set out the instructions for cording the whole of a spring seat, in case you should want to renew a chair entirely, as set out in Chapter Two.

Your cording is going to be laid as follows:

(a) Taking your line from front to back, your cord is attached with a tack to the front frame opposite the front spring nearest the *left-hand edge* (if you are right-handed) with a dangling free end of about 25 cm. (10 ins).

(b) The cord is tied around the *second coil from the top* of the *front* of the front spring, tight enough to compress it by about $2\frac{1}{2}$ cm (1 in).

(c) It is then tied to the *back* of the *top coil of the same spring*, which is also compressed so that the top of the spring is level. All springs are compressed on tying in this way, and the tops of all of them must be level.

(d) It is then tied to the *front and back of the top coil* of each succeeding spring until you reach the one from the last in that row.

(e) The last spring is corded in a reverse manner to the first, i.e. the cord being knotted around the *top coil* on the side nearest to you, and to the *second from the top* on the furthest side. The cord is then tacked to the back framework, and a 25 cm. (10 in) free end left dangling.

To sum up, springs are corded on both sides of the top coil, except for the first and last in each row, which is tied in the second coil on the side nearest the framework.

If you have a row of six springs, your cording would go as follows:

1st Spring Tack cord to framework edge, leave 25 cm. (10 in.) free. On the outer spring, knot to the front of *second coil*, knot to the back of *top coil*, passing the cord over the top of the coil.

2nd Spring Knot to front of top coil. Knot to back of top coil.

3rd Spring Knot to front of top coil. Knot to back of top coil.

4th Spring Knot to front of top coil. Knot to back of top coil.

5th Spring Knot to front of top coil. Knot to back of top coil.

6th Spring Knot to front of top coil. Knot to back of second coil, passing the cord over the top of the coil. Tack cord to framework edge, leaving a 25 cm. (10 in.) free end.

The knot used in cording is a half hitch, which simply means that you pass the cord around the relevant piece of spring, and then pass one end of the cord under the other. It is not necessary to make a 'proper' knot, and it is not desirable, because should your cording be too loose, or too tight, you would not be able to adjust it without completely re-cording. When you have made half hitches, you can make the necessary adjustments by simply removing the framework tack and loosening or tightening as required. Further compression of the spring will slacken the half hitch, which makes it easier to adjust the cord.

With regard to spring compression during cording, the tension on the springs will keep the cording tight, but over-compression may cause the cord to snap. This is a case of learning how much compression is 'just right', and the completion of one set of cording will teach you more than any amount of instruction on the subject.

The free ends of the cord are brought up to knot around the top coils of the first and last springs in each row, and are then tacked down onto the framework.

Even if you only find one broken cord in the chair you are repairing, it is better to renew that cord completely, rather than trying to knot the broken ends, or trying to patch it with a piece of string.

Occasionally you come across a variation in cording pattern, in which case broken cording should be renewed to match the rest. If however you decide to completely renew the cording in a chair of unusual design, it is better to use the method outlined above.

Having restored your springs and webbing, take a piece of hessian of the correct size to stretch to the top of all framework pieces. Turn the edges in, and stretching it tight, half tack it around the frame. When you are satisfied with its position, drive the tacks home.

Half-Tacking

In many upholstering operations, it is advisable to secure fabric, the position of which may have to be altered a few times before it is placed correctly, with tacks that are driven only half way in, so that they can be removed and re-positioned easily. This is known as half-tacking, or temporary tacking, and is a great saving of time and trouble.

Top Stitching

With strong twine and a curved upholstery needle, stitch the tops of the springs to the hessian cover for extra security.

Padding

Your next step will be to replace your padding (which must be teased out to avoid lumpiness) and to add to it if necessary. Or to renew it completely, in which case you will have to make a choice from the types of padding available.

Professionals tend to divide sharply on this matter of padding, some preferring the modern latex or polyesters, while others remain faithful to the more traditional types, such as rubberized hair, coir fibre (made from coconut husks) or curled horse hair.

Latex and Polyesters

These are undoubtedly the cleanest to work with, but have one disadvantage to the beginner, in that they tend to compress too much if you pull the covering material too tight, making the chair uncomfortable, and putting a great deal of strain on the fabric. A certain amount of experimentation is necessary to overcome this, but it is really only a matter of practice, and latex and polyesters are widely used in the profession today.

Always choose those with cavity fillings, i.e. with tiny channels running through them, or with one of the various 'honeycomb' patterns or foamy construction, so that they remain soft and comfortable. The cavities maintain a cool even temperature throughout the chair seat, which would otherwise warm up with body contact, especially in warm weather. Latex and polyesters are allergy-free, an important factor where allergic asthma and allied conditions are concerned.

Your padding is simply cut accurately to size so that it reaches all the outside frames, and its depth should be equal to that of the original padding, as it would have been before it was squashed down with use. You can calculate this depth in your own armchair if you consider that the padding must fit neatly between the back edge of the framework and the bottom of the chair back, and remain uniform throughout the seat.

When the padding is in place, cover it with hessian or unbleached calico or other stout cotton material, half-tacked over the framework edges until you are satisfied (by sitting on it) that the padding is not over-compressed. Then drive the tacks home.

Note
The materials known as 'crumb rubber' and 'foam chips' are not suitable as padding in this instance.

Fibre and Hair Fillings
As mentioned above, the most commonly used are rubberized or curled hair, and coir fibre. Although experts tend to have their favourite materials, there is little to choose between them, and experience will teach you which you prefer.

Whichever you choose, the filling should be teased out so that there are no lumps, and formed into the required shape and size, in this case to fit the chair seat, when the padding must be taken well over to the outer edge of the framework but not beyond it. Throughout upholstery, commonsense decrees that no sharp wooden edges remain to cut into the backs of knees and other portions of the sitter's anatomy except, of course, in the case of show wood, where the wood is left completely bare of upholstery as part of the design.

Fibre Rolls and Rubber Profile

You may have found, on dismembering your chair seat, a long hessian-covered roll along the front framework, tacked into position. This prevents the padding compressing with use to such an extent that the edge of the framework cuts into the back of the sitter's knees. If this roll is in good condition, it can be left in place, but if it is split and/or compressed, it should be removed, and a new one made as follows:

(a) Cut a strip of hessian 8 cm. (3 ins) wide, and long enough to go across the front rail and round both corners with an extra 1 cm. ($\frac{1}{2}$ in.) to spare. Cut on the bias if possible, joining the strip with seams if necessary.

(b) Turn over the edges of the hessian, and tack one edge of it evenly along the front edge of the frame, pulling it taut between tacks. The rest of the hessian should hang down the outside of the frame.

(c) Lay your hair or fibre along the hessian in a long roll about as thick as your middle finger, making sure that it is of equal thickness all along its length.

(d) Fold over your hessian, the edge turned in, and tack it so that the roll overlaps the framework edge by about 1 cm. ($\frac{1}{4}$ in.). Pull tight between tacks, and make sure that the roll is even before placing each succeeding tack.

It is possible to buy rubber profile, a long roll which can be glued or tacked into place, and which represents saving of time and trouble, but is an extra expense. It performs the same function as the fibre roll.

Possibly your chair had a 'hard edge' at the front, in which the actual padding is stitched so that it forms a ridge, instead of a fibre roll. This is often preferred in antique furniture, and we deal with it in the following chapter.

If your chair has a 'spring edge', i.e. a long fairly fine spring around the front, it is best discarded if its condition is not good, and replaced with a fibre roll.

To Apply Seat Padding

(a) Place your padding on the chair seat, bringing plenty up onto the frame edges, and making sure that the whole seat is flat. It must go right up to the outside top edges of the frame, but not over the top, or your final cover will bulge out at the outside of the framework.

(b) Place a layer of wadding or cotton waste on top of the padding, or ends of fibre or hair will work through your covering fabric in time, and this can be very uncomfortable.

(c) Cover the seat with unbleached cotton or calico, stretching it firmly, but not too firmly, or the seat will be hard. (Try sitting on it.) Half-tack it around until you are satisfied, and then drive the tacks home.

(c) Replace your seat cover, which will have already been cut to shape by its original maker, so you will have no difficulty in negotiating the corners. Again half-tack until you are satisfied with its position, and then drive tacks home.

Arms and Backs

If the padding on the inside arms and back has become hard and lumpy, it is sometimes possible to rearrange it with the use of a 'regulator', as illustrated on page 87. If this is not successful, the best course is to remove the appropriate cover pieces and to tease out the padding, adding to it if necessary.

Small Warning Note

If you dismember a chair stuffed with fibre or hair (particularly coir fibre) you will almost certainly find that some of it has broken down into tiny pieces which adhere to your arms. When you finish working, your first impulse is to have a good hot scrub, but this may cause you to develop a rash, especially if you have a tender skin. *First* hold your arms under running cold water, letting the water run from elbow to finger tips, rotating your arms under the stream until all particles are removed.

Suspension Chairs

Small arm chairs, usually known as 'Bridge' or 'TV' chairs,

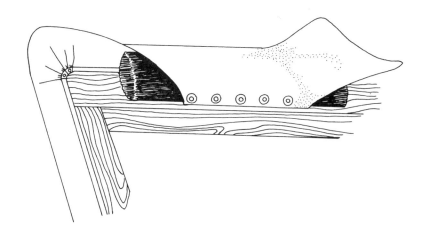

Making a fibre roll

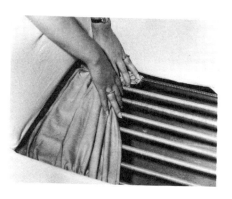

An example of suspension springing, common in small modern chairs.

often have a set of long plastic covered springs with hooks at each end instead of webbing and coil springs. These hooks fit into metal plates on each side of the chair framework. (See illustration.)

These springs slacken with use, and may have to be replaced. The only other likely repair needed is the occasional replacement of a hook at the end of a spring. In certain types of chair, it may be necessary to glue it in, otherwise they simply screw in, although a little plastic wood may be necessary to fill the screw-hole if it has enlarged.

Changing the position of these springs from time to time will prevent overstrain on the centre springs, and prolong the life of the chair.

Structural Repairs

This section possibly belongs at the beginning of the chapter, because the decision to work on or to discard an armchair with actual structural damage must, of course, be taken before you start removing upholstery and reconstructing the chair seat.

However, since many readers may come to this book without the slightest knowledge of the craft of upholstery, and may well read through this chapter simply to see if they consider the idea of reupholstering a chair a viable proposition, basic instructions have been outlined first.

Armchairs are solidly built, and built to last, and actually do stand up to a great deal of abuse without framework damage, but occasionally a leg or back will break, or the seat framework joints loosen, and having loosened, split. Dining-room chairs and other chairs of light construction suffer this type of damage more often, and the instructions set out below apply equally to them.

When intending to deal with a damaged chair, it is as well to have a good think first, because although there is nothing difficult in the methods set out below, they do presuppose some knowledge of carpentry, and a reasonable set of tools. A great deal will depend on the value of the chair, or your affection for it, and obviously an antique chair is almost always worth saving unless it is far gone with woodworm. But if what you have is an ordinary household semi-derelict, it might be as well to discard it in favour of one with a sound frame, which will

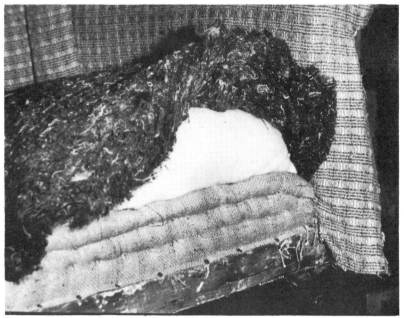

New padding is applied to the seat.

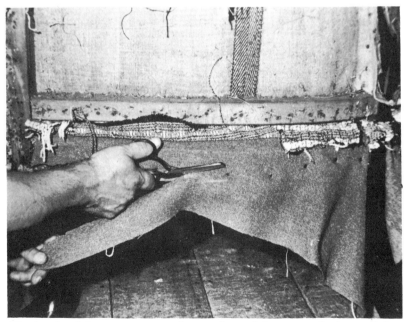

The back of the seat cover is drawn through between the base of the chair back and the top of the seat frame, and tacked down. Excess material is trimmed away. The scraps of old fabric are left to ensure a tight fit.

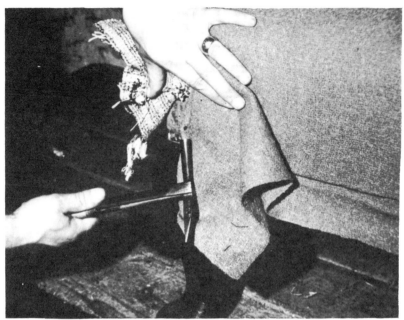

The cover, being folded and tacked into position, first having been back-tacked to the bottom of the front rail.

Before both sides are fully tacked into position, the padding is adjusted and more added if necessary. The excess fabric at the base will be trimmed away, and the hem tacked beneath the bottom of the rail.

Wadding and padding is laid on the inside of the arm.

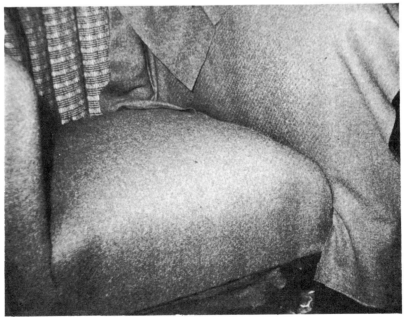

The fabric is positioned for covering the inside arm, drawn well forward to cover the small scroll. The lower edge of the fabric is half-tacked to the bottom rail.

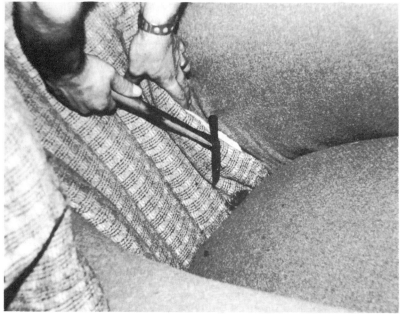

The cover being fastened to the back upright. The old cover and padding on the inside back can be removed for this operation, but keeping it in place ensures a cleaner job, and it is not as difficult as it looks.

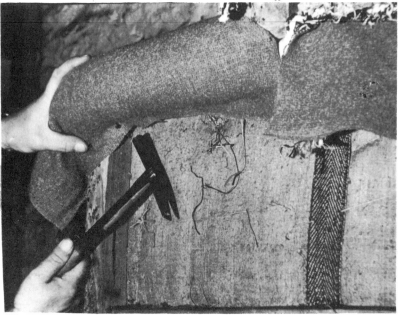

The arm cover is brought over to be tacked beneath the 'bolster'.

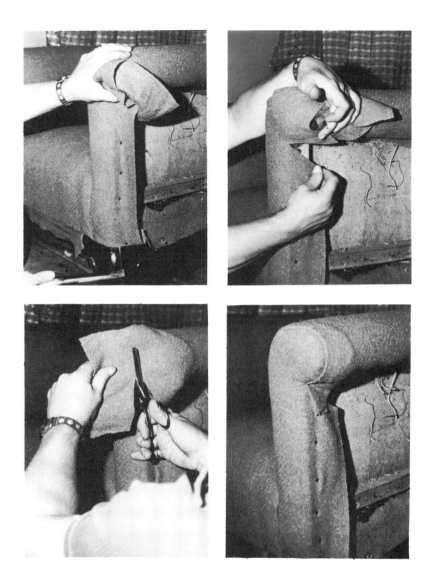

The fabric is brought over and around the scroll, which is too small to need a separate facing.

A vee-cut reduces the bulk of fabric and makes for a neater finish. If a second vee-cut is necessary make it at right angles to the first.

The excess material is trimmed away from the front section.

The completed front arm cover.

probably not cost you more than £1 to £2. However, the point is purely personal, and the proceedures are as follows:

Seat Framework Repairs

Framework pieces are usually joined together with mortice and tenon joints, in which one piece will end in a 'tongue', and the adjacent one in a groove into which the tongue fits. (It is also known, fairly obviously, as a 'tongue and groove' joint.) Sometimes the framework piece will end in a 'dowel pin' which fits into a hole in the adjoining piece, or you may find two dowel pins, one above the other, in which case there will be two holes in the adjoining piece for them to fit into.

Such joints often tend to separate slightly with use, especially if the chair is constantly dragged along the floor. If the chair continues to be used after this separation, the weight of the sitter may cause the tongue or dowel to break, usually in such a way that it remains embedded in the adjoining framework piece. In this case, the repair is a bit more difficult. Joints that have simply separated are easy to deal with.

Separated Joints

(a) Examine the joint for nails, and remove any present.

(b) If the joints are not completely separated, wiggle the two pieces apart, and if this is unsuccessful, tap with a series of little taps (not almighty bangs) on the tongue or dowel piece close to the join. Use a mallet for this, or wrap your hammer head in cloth. Tap a bit, and wiggle a bit until the two parts of the joint come apart. (Heavy hammering will almost certainly break the tongue or dowel, and give you a great deal of extra work.)

(c) If the joint absolutely refuses to budge, try to drive a wedge of hard wood between the dowel or tongue and the adjoining piece, going back to gentle tapping as soon as the joint begins to move.

(d) Once you have separated the pieces, clean out the hole or slot, especially if there is glue in it.

(e) Insert a small quantity of epoxy glue (Araldite is recommended) into the hole or slot, and gently tap the joint back together again.

Epoxy Glues

A word about epoxy glues. They are the very best type of glue to use in this case, because they set rock hard, and make a join which will last for ever. They take twelve hours to set completely, and a week to become absolutely rock hard. During the vital first twelve hours, the joint must not move by as much as a *millimeter* or it may set in the wrong position. (Methylated spirits *may* remove epoxy glue in its early stages, as will scraping with a razor blade, but after that, it is a chisel and sandpaper job, and almost certainly involves wood damage!)

This means that you must place, and support, the joints of the chair in the correct position, and this can be done by first turning the chair upside down, to relieve it of its own weight, and supporting it so that the base of it is absolutely level. Then you must either apply clamps, if you can borrow them from a plumber or carpenter, or bind cords around the four legs up as near to the framework as possible, making a 'tourniquet' with a pencil or piece of stick to increase the tightness. It might seem, at first thought, that wire would be better than cord, as it can be twisted to tightness, but this cuts deeply into the wood, and this well may be 'show wood'.

Your joints must be supported at exactly the correct angle, or your chair will always be a little rickety. Where all four legs are at right angles to the frame and parallel to each other, check the angle of each leg to the frame with a carpenter's square or ordinary geometry set-square. But if the back legs of your chair are angled outwards, and your repair is at the back (where it usually is) make sure that the angles of both legs are equal by cutting a cardboard template when the joint is absolutely in place, and checking with it later in case there has been a slight shift.

Always check within three hours, before the glue has begun to set, and at three-hourly intervals until the glue sets at the twelve hour point.

If you feel that your joints will still need extra reinforcement, cut a hardwood triangle to fit into each framework corner. The sides must fit really flush with the framework sides, and the angle right into the corner, or they are worse than useless. These triangles are screwed into the framework, and must not rise above the top of it.

Broken Dowels

(a) If a dowel has broken, you will almost certainly find half the pin in the dowel hole, and the other half still in the adjacent piece. Both broken pieces will have to be removed in turn, by drilling through the centre of each piece of dowel, and then by gradually enlarging the hole with a small chisel. (Dowel pins are *not* extensions of one framework piece. Both the framework pieces that go to make up the joint have a hole, or two holes, in the centre, and the dowel pin, a tough piece of wood of correct dimensions, goes from the base of one hole to the base of the other.)

(b) Dowelling of the correct size can be bought at hardware stores. If you have an unbroken piece of dowelling, you can take it with you. Otherwise measure the hole with great accuracy. Dowelling comes in standard sizes, and can be sandpapered down if too large. Dowelling that is too small is worse than useless, even if it is glued into position.

(c) Insert the dowel pin into the hole in one framework piece, tapping it gently but firmly with a mallet. If you spread the end with hammering, it won't fit into the corresponding hole. Insert the other end into the hole in the adjacent framework piece, and tap from the other side of the frame. A tiny spot of glue at the base of the hole will strengthen the join, but great gobs of glue will ooze out around the dowel and make an unnecessarily messy job.

The same instructions, of course, apply to mortice and tenon joints.

Broken Legs

These can be considered a major disaster, unless you have some considerable skill in carpentry. Even if epoxy glue never separates, the actual wood may be faulty, possibly affected by woodworm, and the leg may break later in another place. You can glue the break, if the wood is sound, and reinforce it by screwing a wooden 'splint' to the inside of the leg, extending above and below the break, but this is always visible from some angle, unless your upholstery comes below the broken area. Don't spoil the 'line' of the finished chair by incorporating unnecessary frills to hide such repairs. It is better to get another chair.

You can, of course, get new legs made, a comparatively easy job if they are square, but a shaped leg must be turned on a lathe, and this adds to the cost and complication of what set out to be a comparatively easy job.

You alone know the value of the chair involved, but unless this is considerable, it is seldom worth the trouble.

Broken Framework Pieces

The same is true of broken seat or back framework pieces, although these are usually made of unfinished wood, since they are to be covered and won't show. A timber merchant will 'run them off' for you at very little cost, but do remember that you are possibly going to have to fit dowels or tenons, and although this is not particularly difficult, many people find it somewhat of a chore.

Do resist the temptation to apply wooden splints to broken framework pieces. In almost every location, you will be able to feel them however thick the padding, and they can be very uncomfortable indeed. If the back framework is broken, you can't get away with putting the splint at the back, because you will have to apply a great deal of padding to hide it, and the outside back of a chair is normally only padded very lightly, if at all.

Refinishing Show Wood Parts

If the visible wooden parts of your chair (e.g. legs) need refinishing, this is best done when part of the upholstery is removed for convenience when repairing, so that you can keep as much of it as possible out of the way.

Although the modern way to remove existing wood finish is to use stripper, there are two things against it. First, it is very caustic, and may damage your upholstery, and second, it has to be washed off with quantities of cold water, and again your upholstery will be at risk.

Sandpapering may be tedious, but it will turn out to be the best way in the end. Use a medium grade of sandpaper, since a coarse grain will cut into the wood. Fold it in half, or into four, and use the folded edge to work up to the line of your upholstery, and into other awkward places. Refold when necessary.

Once every scrap of the old finish is removed, you may feel that the wood needs re-staining, in which case half-tack a strip of cardboard or folded brown paper exactly to coincide with the edge of your upholstery so that you won't stain the fabric. After the stain is completely dry, apply lacquer or polyurethane coating, again protecting the edge of your fabric.

Castors

Castors usually come in sets of four, so if your chair has one castor missing, you will probably have to buy a set, and may as well replace the lot.

The older type of castor was a 'rod' castor, in which a long rod was fitted into a hole bored into the centre of the bottom of the leg. Now it is possible to buy either rod or plate castors, the latter having a base plate which is screwed onto the bottom of the chair leg. Plate castors are easier to fix, but if your chair originally had rod castors, you are going to have to fill up the hole with plastic wood whatever type of new castors you intend to fix. Short cuts like the filling of the hole with paper to stabilize a loose rod castor are simply not practicable.

Castors fulfill a valuable function in armchairs, since without them, the dragging of a heavy chair can jar the framework and contribute to the loosening of the joints. People who consider that castors flatten the pile of the carpet should remember that chair legs will do this anyway, and that any heavy article of furniture should be moved a few inches occasionally before its weight actually cuts into the pile.

Almost as efficient as castors are 'silent domes', those round raised metal pieces which can be fixed to the base of the legs. They are considered less damaging to carpets than castors, but the chair should still be shifted occasionally.

Base Cover

The last job in your repair work is to turn your chair upside down, and replace the base cover, or make a new one from fine hessian or calico. This may seem an unnecessary step, since the base cover will not be visible when the chair is in use, but it does prevent dust from rising into the chair, and crumbled padding from falling onto the carpet. It also gives a neat finish to your first upholstery project, and your friends, intrigued by your expertise, may well peep underneath to see just how well you have finished the job.

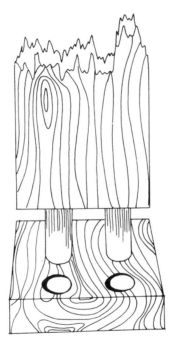

Dowel joint

Chapter Two

From Square One to Infinity

If you decide that the upholstery and padding on your chair are not worth saving, and that you would prefer to strip your chair virtually down to the framework, you will find the task a little more elaborate than the basic repairs outlined in the previous chapter. No single step is difficult, however, and where special expertise is required, this comes with practice.

In this chapter, we give step-by-step instructions for building a chair from its framework. You must make your own rules of flexibility in deciding, for instance, whether to lay new webbing and springs, or whether the existing ones are in good enough condition to leave as they are.

In dismantling your chair, obviously you will have to remove the old upholstery fabric, and it is usually not considered advisable to remove all the old cover in one go, as padding will begin to fall all over the place and make a great deal of mess. Therefore one normally removes the fabric from each location in turn, and new work can be covered with cloth or paper to keep it clean.

It was once a common practice to cover the chair with unbleached cotton or other stout economical material before applying the final fabric covering. This had much to recommend it, as it kept padding well in place, lengthened the life of such fine covering fabrics as satin, and made the future job of reupholstering far easier. (Our ancestors always took the long view.)

The decision whether or not to apply a cotton cover is entirely yours, but if it appears to be an extra and rather unnecessary refinement, it should be remembered that it forms an excellent 'dummy-run' for your final cover. It is far less costly to make a mistake in unbleached cotton than in, say, Dralon or tweed. The cotton cover is applied in exactly the same way as the final fabric, and directions for the latter are applicable to it in every way.

If you make a cotton cover, the old fabric pieces can form a pattern from which to cut your final cover, and if you plan to renew the padding completely (which is not usually necessary) it is permissable to remove all the old cover pieces at once (which can then form the basis for your pattern) as you will be removing the padding as well.

On the other hand, the drafting of a new pattern is not difficult (see page 55) and you may prefer the more usual and cleaner method of uncovering and working on one location at a time.

This information, which may seem out of context, is given here because many people can't wait to get the tatty old upholstery out of the way, or have some idea of 'stripping the decks for action', only to find that unnecessary problems have been created.

It is also a good idea to form a plan at this stage as to your intentions regarding the finished chair. Before you start even the most elementary of first steps decide whether or not you will lay a cotton cover, whether seams will be piped or not, if you intend buttoning or fluting the back, how you will deal with the fronts of the arms, etc. Plans can be changed if they later appear impractical, but there is something slightly terrifying in standing in front of a dismantled chair with knotted brow wondering what to do next. More upholstery projects are abandoned from lack of forward planning than for any other reason.

(1) Renewing the Seat

If the webbing and seat are in good condition, there is little virtue in renewing them, and even if a complete replacement is required, you will already possess the basic knowledge if you have read Chapter One.

However, there are two variations on the webbing theme, you can either a) leave your webbing in a continuous roll, cutting off each piece after it is stretched and tacked down. Or b) cut it into the required lengths before starting, each measuring from one frame edge to the other, plus four inches. Many people find it easier to work with short pieces, finding that the roll gets rather in the way.

In either case:

(a) Fold the edge of the webbing under, and tack it to the top of the frame, first with one tack in the centre, and then with two more below it, to make a triangle.

(b) Stretch the webbing across to the opposite side of the frame, straining it over the framework with the webbing stretcher held well down, and while it is still stretched, fasten it to the top of the frame with three tacks, as described above.

(c) Fold over the edge of the webbing (cutting it off if you are using a continuous roll) and secure it with two tacks.

(d) Continue to place webbing pieces across the framework, the distance between the pieces approximately the same as the width of the webbing . . . certainly not wider.

(e) After completing the webbing in one direction (normally from front to back) attach webbing in the transverse direction, weaving in and out of the completed webbing, in a weaving or darning pattern.

Springing

(a) Sew the bottom of each spring onto the top side of the webbing where two webbing pieces cross. Using a curved needle and strong twine, securely stitch the base of the spring to the webbing in at least four places. Finish off by knotting both ends of twine beneath the webbing.

(b) Cord the springs, if necessary, following the instructions on page 17.

(c) Cover the whole seat with a piece of hessian, half-tacking it to the framework, then driving home the tacks when you are satisfied that it is correct. If any springs rear their ugly heads, they are incorrectly corded, and this is the time to do them again.

(d) Using a curved needle, stitch the tops of the springs to the hessian cover.

Seat Cover

Even if you intend to make a fitted cushion, you will need to pad the chair seat, which can be done with a piece of plain latex

The webbing is tacked into position on the framework edge.

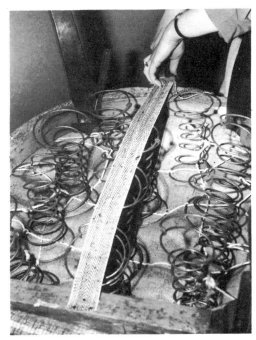

The webbing, tacked at one end, is stretched across the centre row of springs, and tightened over the edge with a webbing stretcher.

Close-up of webbing stretcher in use.

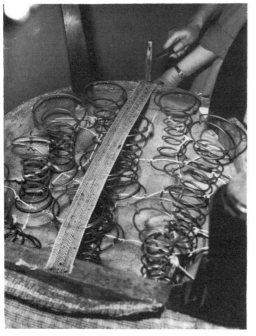

The webbing end is tacked into place, while still being stretched.

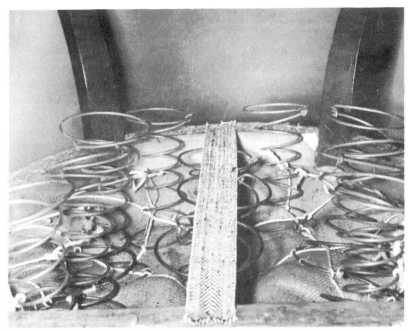

Showing the compression of the centre springs by the webbing, in contrast to the surrounding springs.

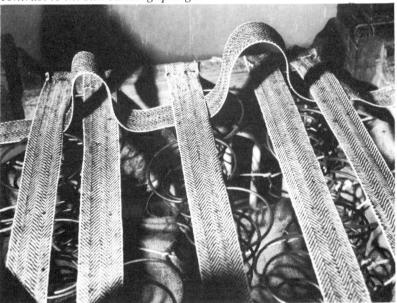

Once the webbing is laid from front to back, pieces are laid from side to side, interwoven. It is important to follow the lines of the springs.

The completed webbing.

Stitching will keep the webbing pieces in place. Note how the thread is twisted around the curved needle.

foam cut to size, but for real durability, it is better to use fibre or hair.

For comfort and good wear, you should place a fibre roll or rubber profile along the top edge of your framework, but you may prefer to sew a 'hard edge', which serves the same purpose.

Using a Fibre Roll or Rubber Profile

(a) Using fibre or hair, tease it out to make sure it is even and without lumps.

(b) Place your fibre roll or rubber profile along the top edge of the framework (see page 24), and place a layer of padding about 3 inches deep all over the seat, and packed well against it, because you will need plenty of firmness at the front, the area of greatest pressure. Carry the padding well up to the edges of the framework at the back and sides, but not beyond the top outer edge.

(c) Cover the padding with a layer of wadding, and then stretch a piece of fine hessian or unbleached muslin over, half-tacking it to the framework on all sides, tacking down when you are satisfied that it is smooth and taut. Check that your padding goes right to the framework edges before tacking down.

(d) With a straight upholstery needle, sew through material and padding with a bridle stitch, i.e. long stitches at short intervals. A few well spaced lines running from front to back or from side to side will be sufficient to keep the padding in place.

Building a Hard Edge

We illustrate the professional method of building a hard edge, and although this is not particularly difficult (the operator completed it in about ten minutes) a certain expertise is necessary, and this comes with practice. For those who find the idea intimidating, we set out a far easier method, although the results cannot be said to be so satisfactory.

(a) Cut your hessian or unbleached cotton for the seat cover with at least an extra six inches at the lower edge to accommodate the extra padding used.

(b) Tease out your padding, and lay it on the seat, building it up at the front.

(c) Turning under the edges of the hessian, half-tack it into position on all sides, leaving an area on one side of the front into which you can get your hand to add more padding if necessary. (It is usually necessary!)

(d) Introduce more padding, as shown in the illustration, making sure that it is packed tightly and evenly at the front.

(e) Make a roll two or three inches deep by sewing a seam, using a long needle and upholstery thread, along the top front edge, making sure that the padding inside the roll is tight and even. This could be described as 'sewing a fibre roll' at the top front edge, with the difference that this is an integral part of the seat itself, and not applied separately.

Choice of Fabric

In the interests of forward planning this is the moment to consider your choice of material, how to draft a pattern, and how to calculate from that pattern the amount of fabric you will need.

If you are considering the upholstering of an antique piece, it makes obvious good sense to restrict the choice of fabric to those approximating the original. This is not simply purism, but an acknowledgement of the fact that the piece was originally designed to be complimented by the materials of the day, and never seems to look its best in the modern idiom. The possible exception is Dralon velvet, which approximates the old-fashioned velvets fairly closely, and has many advantages in use.

If your antique chair still has the remnants of its original upholstery, this will enable you to buy its modern equivalent, but if at some time it has been upholstered 'out of context', almost any book on antiques, or a glance around an antique shop, will give the clue to the correct choice of fabric.

We require a number of things from our upholstery fabric, only one of which is the need to like it, because we are going to live with it for a long time. We need the colour and pattern (if we choose a patterned fabric) to blend, harmonize or contrast cleverly with our existing decor. We expect the material to wear satisfactorily, to resist fading, to be easy to keep clean. If we want something that won't show the dirt, we may have to

Building a Hard Edge

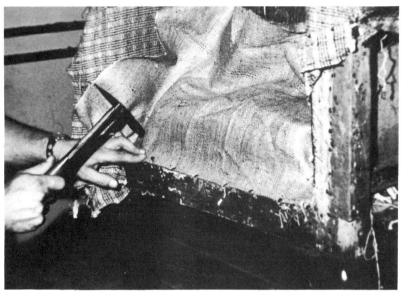

The ends of the hessian are tucked securely into the sides of the seat, and the front edge, hem tucked under, is tacked to the front of the framework.

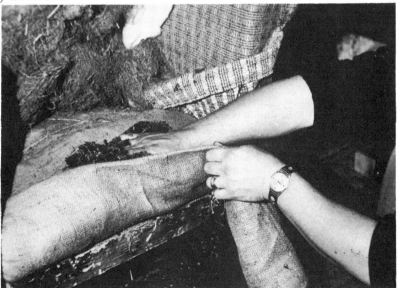

The hessian is folded over and pulled taut while padding is introduced, and pushed well down to the front.

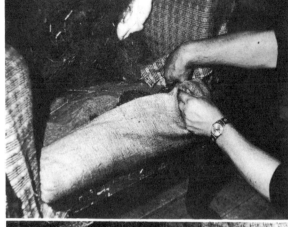

The padding must be firm and even along both length and depth.

The hessian of the hard edge is stitched to the cover, using a curved needle. The twist of thread around the needle will ensure a tight firm stitch.

A curved needle facilitates sewing where the needle cannot be drawn through the work and brought back to make a neat short stitch.

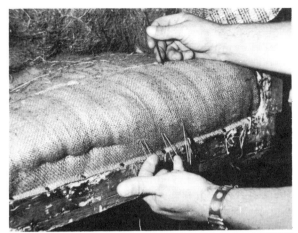

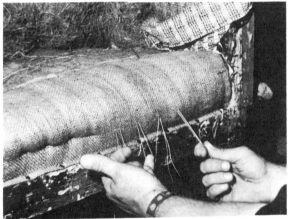

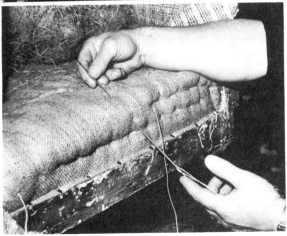

This stitching keeps the padding from shifting. Starting with the end of the thread wound round a tack placed in the framework, the loops are made by drawing the needle from a position half way up the hard edge front, diagonally upwards to emerge near the top seam. A mattress needle is used.

The thread is not drawn out at the top, the needle being retracted to emerge at the front. The loops, held in the fingers during the operation, are pulled tight, the thread compressing the padding inside evenly.

To stitch the top of the hard edge, the needle is drawn as shown, from front to back.

The needle is withdrawn, and re-enters and emerges behind but level with the previous sites of entry and exit.

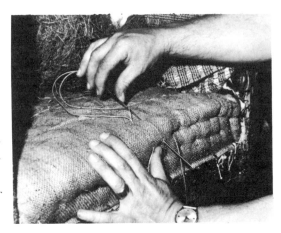

The thread is wound several times around the point of the needle.

The thread is drawn tightly, resulting in a firm recessed knot.

sacrifice other advantages, particularly decorative interest, in favour of a dark colour. In these days of spray-on dry cleaners, however, many things, including armchairs, are easier to keep clean than a generation ago, although the factor should still be borne in mind when choosing a fabric.

If you need a specially hard-wearing fabric, this is another factor, and where cost is to be borne in mind, the choice may once again be limited. Upholstery fabrics, never cheap, should never be an impulse buy, as you will need about $5\frac{1}{2}$ metres (6 yds.) for the average armchair, and a wrong choice makes a great hole in anybody's budget.

Should you incline towards a patterned fabric, never choose from a small snippet, but ask to see the material draped over a chair, or at least the shop counter. Patterns can change alarmingly when you see repeat after repeat after repeat. Remember that patterns and stripes must match up, as they do in dressmaking, and you may need extra material. Get the salesman to advise you.

Patterned Fabrics

Chintz	A printed cotton fabric with a glazed surface which should be virtually permanent. (Ask about this when buying.) Often used for reupholstering Victorian pieces. Usually patterned with flowers and leaves, more often stylized than in faithful reproduction, and often in delicate and pastel colours. Medium to high price range, according to quality. Good wearing quality, although even 'permanent' glaze tends to wear off as time progresses. Unglazed chintz is also available.
Cretonne	A stronger material, unglazed, in a variety of designs, usually bold and colourful. Medium to high price range. Wearing quality good.
Brocade	Multi-coloured jacquard pattern fabric in cotton, silk, wool or nylon, varying greatly in price and quality, but

	usually smooth and hard-wearing. Beware of a very thin brocade; it can't be expected to give good service.
Brocatelle	Brocade with a raised pattern, again varying in price and quality.
Damask	A flatter, reversible type of brocade, usually more expensive, sometimes very expensive indeed. Usually wears very well, and is available in a very wide range of colours and patterns, some quite lovely.
Moquette	A little old-fashioned, but still used 'in the trade' and seldom available in retail shops. Either 'cut' or 'uncut' according to whether the surface loops are severed or left intact, it wears just about for ever, and the chances are that the original material you peeled off your armchair was moquette.
Tweed	Exhibiting weaves of mixed colour rather than patterns, all good tweeds make excellent chair coverings, and are available in great variety. You often do better in the coat material department than in soft furnishings. Very bulky tweeds are not always easy to work with, and open weaves obviously don't wear as well as the closer weaves. Price according to quality.

Plain Fabrics

| Dralon Velvet | Considered one of the best modern upholstery fabrics, fadeless and washable (it can virtually be scrubbed *in situ*), and available in a reasonable range of plain colours. Since one measures the wearing quality of upholstery fabric in decades, we don't yet know for how long Dralon will last, as it is a |

comparatively new fabric, but we haven't heard of anyone reporting signs of wear. Tends to be expensive.

Velvet — Available in glorious colours, but of doubtful wearing quality, and most velvets crush badly. Not cheap, either.

Corduroy — Less expensive, less crushable, wears well, good colour range if you search a bit, but rather narrow in width. (See paragraph on the use of narrow materials.) Upholstery corduroy is also available. Price reasonable.

Plush — With a longer and less dense pile than velvet, plush tends to be prickly and therefore a little uncomfortable. Expensive, too, but gives your chair a very rich look. (Hence the term 'plushy'.)

Velour — A very smooth fabric, often in glorious soft colours, but can be prohibitively expensive.

Satin — Much used in antique chairs, especially when it comes in Regency or Victorian stripes. Also available in patterns. *Not* for ordinary home wear and tear, and not particularly comfortable, as it tends to be slippery. Prices vary widely according to quality.

Sateen — A not-very-satisfactory version of the above, and not always easy to use, as it tends to fray with tacking and stitching. Price very reasonable.

Denim — Narrow in width, but with great possibilities where family homes are concerned, because it is both cheap and virtually indestructable. Good range of colours if you search a bit, including black and brown, either of which look well in a contemporary setting. Price very reasonable.

Leather, suede and P.V.C. are not recommended for beginners, because working with them is really an expert's job. It is really not worth paying the price expected for these materials until you can be sure of doing an expert job. P.V.C. is reasonably cheap but the seams really should be heat welded, and only a professional has the necessary equipment and technical knowledge.

If you intend to finish your chair with braid or ruching (see page 90) it is as well to buy this when you choose your upholstery fabric. The colour range in trimmings is fairly wide, but it can be extremely irritating to upholster your chair with a view to embellishment, only to find that you can't get the match or contrast you want.

Modern chairs are seldom trimmed in this way, although buttoning and the piping of seams are often used. Older chairs were often embellished to avoid back-tacking, in which the tacks are hidden, the visible tack line being hidden with braid or ruching. Since back-tacking is an easy operation, and only omitted by professionals because of the extra time involved, there is no reason whatsoever for you to embellish your chair simply because it was done in the first place, if you prefer a clean finish.

Those conversant with dressmaking will not need to be told that whatever material you use, it should all be 'cut one way' with regard to both breadth and length. There may seem to be no difference when the material is held in the hand or slung across a table, but most fabrics have a 'nap' running one way only, and deviations would show up on the actual finished chair.

If you are using a patterned fabric, obviously the pattern must be the right way up throughout, and the chair will have a more balanced look if the bottom of a pattern 'block' is placed in the centre of the front of the seat, in the centre of the bottom of the inside back, and on the tops of the arms. Drape your uncut fabric to try the effect before cutting, and make sure that you take this into consideration when you cut out your pattern pieces.

Stripes should coincide when two adjoining pieces come together, and all stripes should run in the same direction, usually *down* the chair, rather than across it.

Pattern Layout

Inside wing · Inside back · Inside arm · Outside wing · Front arm panel · Outside arm · Cushion front · Piping · Seat front · Flounce

Using the diagram on the right list the pieces you are going to need to cover your chair and then fill in the measurements of each piece as you take them. Take the width measurements first, making sure they are across the widest points. In some instances you will not require all the pieces shown here, depending on the style of the chair.

Transfer measurements to paper pattern and mark allowances on each for seams etc., as follows –

10–15 mm ($\frac{1}{2}$–$\frac{3}{4}$ inches) for seams and tacking to exposed wood surfaces.

50 mm (2 inches) for attachment of stretchers or pullers.

10 mm (4 inches) for pulling the fabric around frame edges and tacking.

To estimate the amount of material needed, add up the length in meters or yards and add 900 mm or 1 yard to the final figure to find the total material required.

Pin paper patterns to length of fabric as shown in layout diagram, taking care to centre any design on fabric. Ensure the nap runs downwards, except in the case of the seat which should have the nap running towards the front. After you have pinned all the pieces onto the fabric cut them out.

Cushion top	Cushion bottom			
Right outside arm	Fnt.piece	Sidepiece	Sidepiece	
Left outside arm				Fnt. seat
Inside back	Skirt flounce			
Outside back				
Right inside arm				
Left inside arm				
Piping				

Use of Narrow Fabric

If your material is too narrow to cover the widest part of the chair (usually the back) always centre the fabric on the area, and seam extra widths of fabric on each side, possibly piping the seams to make this look part of the intentional design. (Fabric is usually used with its *length* going down from top to bottom of the chair.) A wide plain chair back invites fluting (see page 81) which means that small pieces of material of cut fabric can be used. If you prefer a plainer back, a little extra padding on each side of the side seams (described above) will recess the seams and add to the 'intentional' look.

If you have a modern chair, in which the back is right-angled at all corners, you can often achieve a smart effect by creating a square centre panel, with added pieces of similar size at the top and bottom in addition to the two sides. The seams are then recessed with padding.

Saving on Fabric

If you are a little short on fabric, there are two economy measures that you can try.

(a) If you have a loose cushion, you can cover the underside of it with another fabric, as it will be hidden. The cushion in this case will have to fit very well between the chair arms, or your deception will show. The cushion will, of course, be non-reversible.

(b) When making your inside arm cover, substitute hessian or unbleached cotton for the bottom portion, where it will be hidden by the seat and cushion. These pieces are known as 'flies' and are often used in the trade. Make sure that they are well hidden, as they can ruin the look of a chair if they are visible.

You may not consider it worth the trouble to indulge in these 'tricks' to save about a yard of material, but they can prove extremely useful if you find that you have underestimated your fabric requirements, and can't get more to match.

Drafting a Pattern

Patterns are drafted on thin paper (preferably in a continuous roll) or on old sheets or other cotton material, which is easier to manage.

Start drafting your pattern by measuring each part of the chair across its widest and then its longest line. Draw a rectangle to these measurements on your paper or cotton cloth, using a felt pen, and write in the centre of each rectangle the portion of the chair's anatomy to which it belongs.

This should be done strictly in the order laid down in the diagram, or you may land up buying more fabric than you really need.

Remember that you must leave enough at the sides and top and bottom of each piece for the edges to be turned under . . . at least half an inch everywhere.

And that:

(a) The inside back cover must reach from *over the top of the top rail* to *underneath the bottom rail*, and *over both side rails*. (Remember about buttoning and fluting, too.)

(b) The inside arm cover must reach to the *underside of the bottom rail, over the top of the arm* and to the *edge of the front of the arm* in a straight-armed chair, well forward in the case of a scroll arm.

(c) The seat cover must be stretched to the rails on all four sides.

(d) The front seat cover must reach *below the bottom rail* in front, and round the sides of the seat, between the edge of the seat and the inside arm for at least four inches.

(e) The outside back cover must stretch from the *outside of the top rail,* to *under the bottom of the bottom rail.*

(f) The outside arms must be covered from the *top of the arm* in a straight-armed chair, and to the *bottom of the bolster* in a scroll-armed chair. Your fabric must go to the *back of the back upright*, and to the *front of the front upright*, or around the front, according to the type of chair.

If you lay out your rectangles as shown in the diagram, this will give you the amount of fabric you will need to buy. If you intend fluting, buttoning or piping seams, you should turn to the next chapter for details, as you will need more fabric.

Shaping the Pattern

Take each rectangle, and hold it onto the appropriate site on the chair. Mark the paper or cloth with a felt pen to the shape of that particular part, remembering to allow for turnings. Remember that corresponding pieces, e.g. two inside arms, two outside wing covers, are *not* identical, but are mirror-images of each other. When cutting your fabric, you cannot cut both pieces from one pattern, or one will ultimately show its underside to the world.

Cut your pattern pieces to shape.

When pinning your pattern onto the fabric, do so in the order and position shown in the diagram. If you do it any other way, you may find that you do not have enough material.

Back-Tacking

Before we go on to the actual methods of applying the fabric cover, there is one technique which must be explained, and that is back-tacking. This is a method of laying a line of tacks so that they cannot be seen when finished, and is most commonly used at the bottom edge of the seat front, where ordinary tacking would be very visible.

Back-tacking is also often used on the top edge of the outside arm cover, especially in a straight-armed chair, where, again, the tack line would be visible. In a scroll-armed chair, the tacks would normally be obscured by the bolster of the scroll.

The back-tacking of the outside back cover down the length of one side will obviate the necessity of stitching down *two* seams when the cover has been placed, leaving only one to be stitched. This represents a personal choice . . . whether you prefer sewing or back-tacking.

The edge to be back-tacked is tackled *first* in placing any cover piece, as the rest of the fabric must be free. Once one edge has been back-tacked, you cannot back-tack another edge on the same piece of fabric.

The technique of back-tacking obviates the need for covering an ugly tack line with braid, a method sometimes resorted to by cheap manufacturers who grudge the small amount of extra time required for back-tacking. Braid should only be used when it adds to the decorative value of the chair, and not as a time-saver.

(a) Take your piece of fabric, the edge folded in, and lay the edge of it along your proposed tack line, *the back of the fabric towards you*. Make sure that the edge coincides absolutely with its desired final position, usually the bottom edge of the front seat rail.

(b) Tack one edge of it, through the turned-in edge, at one end, and, stretching it taut, place only enough tacks to keep the fabric in position. (Four or five, according to the width you are working on.)

(c) Cut a cardboard strip about 1 cm ($\frac{1}{2}$ in) wide, with an absolutely straight lower edge, and as long as the length to be back-tacked. Pieces of cardboard strip can be joined as the bottom edges coincide *absolutely*.

(d) Place your cardboard along and fractionally below your existing tacks, making sure that it is dead level all the way along. Tack it down with your tacks about 2.5 cm (1 in) apart, making sure that no tack-head goes below the bottom edge of the cardboard.

(e) Fold back the rest of the fabric, and the edge will present itself sharp and neat, the tacks completely hidden. The rest of the cover piece can now be tacked into its appropriate position.

Neat Finishes in Awkward Places

Before we deal with the actual covering of a chair, it might be as well to discuss the methods of taking your fabric neatly around a corner or a rail.

Where a corner is sufficiently 'wide', e.g. in a high curved chair back, the necessary pleats will be small, and when tacked, will lie quite flat, but a tighter corner may need special treatment.

Pleating a Round Corner

Working from the back, we will consider a juncture at right-angles of two framework rails, the top of which is rounded out by padding.

(a) Pull the fabric over the corner, making sure that you

Pleating Corners

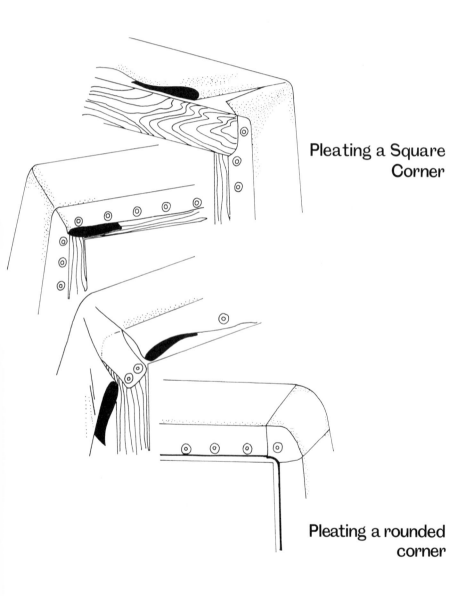

Pleating a Square
Corner

Pleating a rounded
corner

have equal amounts of fabric on both sides. The fabric edge should reach almost to the bottom right-angle joint of the two rails.

(b) Place two tacks close together in the edge of the fabric just above this joint, and make a pleat on each side of these tacks, running inwards towards the corner above.

(c) Cut along the *inside* of these pleats, stopping short of the corner, or the cut will be visible from the other side.

(d) Fold under the cut edges of the pleats, and bring them together so that the bottom points coincide. Tack down to the frame rail. The centre fabric piece can be trimmed if it is too bulky.

Pleating a square corner

(a) Pull the fabric over the corner, as directed above.

(b) Tack the fabric edge to the bottom of the rail along both sides to within approx. 5 cm. (2 in.) of the joint itself.

(c) Form pleats in these untacked spaces, cut them up towards the corner, fold in the edges, trim away excess fabric on both sides of the centre.

(d) Bring together the folded-in edges, so that they lie side by side, and tack them down their length.

Fitting Around a Rail

When your rail comes right at a corner, half-tack your cover to within about five inches of the rail, folding the corner of the cover back at the rail corner.

Make a V-cut from the centre of the fabric towards the inside corner of the rail, snipping gradually until, with the edge folded under, it will fit neatly around the rail.

When the rail, although flush with the back of the chair, is recessed in from the side (as when the seat is wider than the back) you will need to cut your fabric towards the *centre* of the rail, and within a few centimetres of the rail itself, and then to extend two small V-cuts, one to each corner of the rail. If you feel the slightest bit doubtful about this operation, try it on a piece of scrap material first, but in actual fact it is not difficult.

The Real Upholstery Bit

Having padded and covered the seat, we now proceed to pad

and cover the other parts of the *inside* of the chair, namely, the inside arms and inside back.

Straight Arms

These present no problem, and possibly the best guide is to study the way it was done before. If the top of the arm is very wide, you will need a separate cover piece to go along it, and another to face the front of the arm, which should be laid last, after both inside and outside covers have been fixed. Such seams are often piped, as this gives a more pleasing finish.

Either polyesters or natural fibres can be used to pad the inside and top of the arm.

Scroll Arms

(1) Using Polyesters or Latex Foam

(a) Lay a nice plump swathe of wadding or cotton waste on the inside and along the top of the arm.

(b) Fix a fibre roll or rubber profile along the *top front edge* of the scroll, so that it hangs over in front of the frame for about 1 cm. ($\frac{1}{2}$ in.).

(c) Cut a sheet of foam to the length of the *inside arm frame*, sufficient to go from the bottom rail, up over the bolster to its underside where it joins the outside arm. In depth it must reach from the *inside of the fibre roll* or profile to the *back of the arm* where it joins the inside back upright.

(d) Half-tack the bottom of the foam sheet to the *bottom rail of the inside arm frame*, and take it up the inside arm and over the bolster, half-tacking it there. Make sure that it fits right up to the inner edge of your fibre roll or profile at the front, and right along the arm to reach the edge of the back frame where it joins the back of the arm.

(e) Make sure that the foam is smooth and even, and not over-stretched in any place. Do not allow it to hang below the bottom rail, trimming it off at the frame edge if necessary after the rest of the foam is tacked into place.

Using Hair or Fibre Padding (As Illustrated)

(a) Tease out your padding, and lay it evenly, lining the inside arm and taking the padding up over the scroll, keeping it in place with skewers if necessary. Make sure you take the pad-

The inside arm cover is brought forward over the top of the scroll as well as to the front, and is secured by half-tacking.

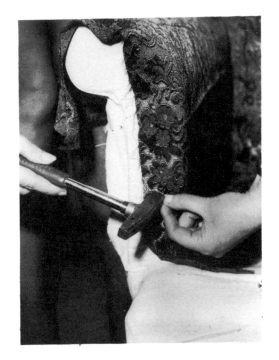

The gap is not important, as it will be covered by the front facing.

The fabric is pleated by hand, and each pleat tacked into position.

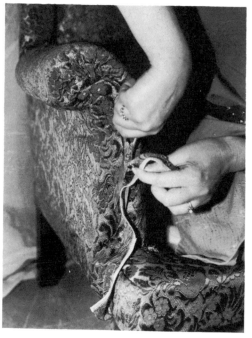

The outside arm cover, attached to the bottom and back rails, is brought forward to the front of the arm, and tacked into position. Excess fabric is trimmed away.

The shaped facing is hemmed by machine. A cardboard template can be cut to use as a pattern.

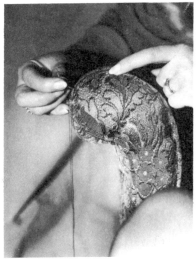

Wadding, cut to the shape of the scroll arm facing, is placed into position, and the facing pinned over it.

The facing is stitched on, using a curved needle.

ding up to the frame edges, but not beyond them. Either pad lightly over the scroll, tapering off within about 5 cm. (2 in.), or remember to tease down a little padding before pleating your cover over. (Padding doesn't stay particularly easily in that position, and you have nothing to skewer it to.)

(b) Place your cover fabric in position, and tack along the framework under the bolster (where the tack line will be hidden by the top edge of the outside arm cover, which you will be applying later), right along from the front edge of the arm to the back where it reaches the back upright. Tack the bottom edge of the fabric (remembering to turn in all edges) beneath the bottom rail. Bring the fabric to the front, and tack it on both sides from a midway line down to the bottom of the arm front. Do not tack over the top front of the scroll.

(c) Pleat the material over the front of the scroll, smoothing the pleats with a regulator if you find it helpful . . . the flat 'eye' is designed for this purpose. Make sure your pleats are neat and even.

(d) Place a tack in the centre of the base of each pleat.

(e) Cut a cardboard template the exact size and shape of the arm front to serve as a pattern for the facing, cut out your facing and proceed as illustrated on page 62.

We also illustrate on page 29 the correct proceedure for covering an arm with a scroll so small that the use of a facing might well give a clumsy-looking result. The decision as to which method to choose is made easier if you drape and swathe uncut material as an experiment.

Inside Wings

If you are working on a wing chair, the next step is to cover the inside wings. Where the wings are continuous with the arms, as is occasionally the case, you can pad the inside arms and inside wings in one operation, and cut the inside cover in one piece.

If the wings have an open framework, cover them with hessian or unbleached cotton inside and out.

Padding

Whether using natural fibres or polyester, the depth of the wing padding should be sufficient to make a tight fit between the base of the wing and the top of the arm (which has already been padded) allowing just enough room for the wing cover fabric.

This usually presupposes a padding depth of about 5 cm. (2 in.) all over, since the depth must be consistent.

(1) Using Polyester or Latex

Carry the foam over the frame, tacking it to the *back*, upright.

(2) Using Natural Fibres

Pad right across the wing, carrying the padding over the *outer* edge of the framework. Cover with wadding or cotton waste.

Covering Inside Wings

Where the wing covers are applied separately (there is an alternative method on page 73), the front cover is brought over the edges of the wing frame and tacked there, the fabric being pleated as necessary to negotiate a smooth corner (see illustration on page 59), and each pleat tacked separately. The inside edge of the wing cover is then stitched to the back upright.

If you have the required tight fit between the base of the wing and the top of the arm, the fabric should stay in position.

Inside Back

Whether you are using polyesters or natural fibres, your padding will have to reach from below seat level to the *back* of the top rail, as with wings. When using polyesters, your foam sheet must reach behind the seat to be tacked onto the bottom rail, and *must* be wide enough to cover the inside back at its widest part. (It is not practicable to try to make joins.)

When using natural fibres, pad generously and absolutely evenly, because the inside back is the 'show-piece' of any armchair, and the most visible to critical onlookers.

Remember the necessity for a tight fit between the inside back padding and the back of the seat, to prevent the padding from working down later. Even if you decided against making a cotton cover, it is a very good idea to cover the inside back with unbleached cotton and to fasten it down as you would the final cover. A few rows of bridle-stitching across the width will make sure that the padding stays in place.

Applying the Cover

(a) Drape the fabric over the inside of the chair, taking it, edge turned under, *over the top of the top rail*, and half-tacking it down. Pleat at corners if necessary, and half-tack each pleat down.

(b) Take the fabric down between bottom of the inside back and the back of the seat, pulling it smooth, and making sure that there are no creases. Half-tack it beneath the bottom rail.

(c) Half-tack it to both side frames, taking the fabric to the back of the rails.

(d) When quite satisfied, drive tacks home.

Outside Back, Arms and Wings

You may be advised that these can be left unpadded, and simply covered with upholstery fabric, and indeed you may find that this was originally done on the chair on which you were working.

But even if you carry your padding over the outside edges of the back and wings, (which helps the fabric to hang better, as well as avoiding a sharp-edged look), you may still find that you get a rather meagre appearance if your fabric is merely stretched from side to side with no backing.

Therefore, padding in the form of thin polyester foam, or felt, can be stretched from one edge to the other across the outside back and wings, and tacked into position before the cover is applied.

Outside Arms

Because of the many variations in chair design, it is not feasible to give specific directions for all types, but you can start by back-tacking either along the front edge, or the top edge, whichever is the most convenient. (Remember that you can turn and support your chair so that it presents a convenient working surface.) The top edge will meet and just overlap the top of the inside arm cover, and will be beneath the bolster in a scroll-armed chair. The edge that is not back-tacked will be stitched as a final operation, as a tack-line would be visible, and this may influence your choice as to where to back-tack.

The back of the wing, showing the fastening of the front wing cover over the top rail. Note that the padding is carried well over and then 'tailed off', and that the fabric at the corners is pleated and tacked down.

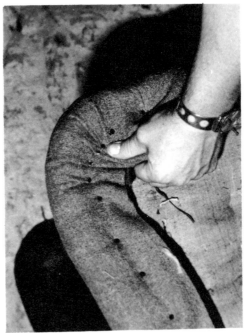

Close-up of corner pleating.

Fixing the back cover, with half-tacking at the bottom, and with skewers at the top.

In this case, the outside wing covers are made continuous with the outside arm cover to save extra unnecessary seaming. The varying designs of chairs and width of fabric dictate where this would be expedient.

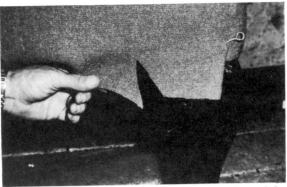

The final touches—although the front edge of the seat was back-tacked, this cannot be carried above the legs. The fabric at the outside edges is vee-cut and folded under.

Ornamental brass-or bronze-headed studs can be used here, or ordinary tacks can be covered with braid. Personal tastes and the design and period of the chair are the best guides to choice.

Where seam stitching is effected (as here where the outside of the bottom arm is stitched to the side of the seat) the curved needle is drawn first through the edge of one side and then through the edge of the other. When drawn together, the stitches should be invisible.

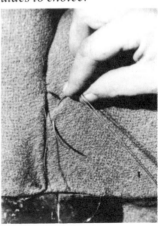

The back edge of the cover will be hidden by the edge of the outside back cover, and can therefore be tacked. It is carried round to the *back* of the frame.

The bottom of the cover is tacked beneath the bottom rail. Half-tack (with the exception of your back-tacked line) until you are satisfied that the cover fits correctly, and then drive the tacks home.

Outside Back Cover

This is the last operation in fitting the cover, and no part of the outside back cover should be visible from the front. Inside arm, wing and back covers have all been taken round to the back of the top and side rails, and the outside back cover over- laps these cover edges to stop short at the top edge of the *backs* of the respective rails.

In fitting the back cover, it is essential that the fabric should 'fall' correctly, especially if it is striped or patterned, when the slightest crookedness is very noticable. Half-tack until you are completely satisfied, especially if you decide to back-tack along the top or down one side, after which the fall of the fabric cannot easily be rectified.

If your chair has a straight top edge, this can be back-tacked, but a curved or scrolled-top makes this out of the question, and you should back-tack down one side if possible. Back- tacking gives good 'purchase' from which to stretch the rest of the cover, the remaining seams of which should be stitched.

An Alternative Method of Covering Wings and Backs

We have left discussion of this alternative method of covering wings and backs until this point to avoid confusion, and refer to the illustrations on page 75.

It is possible to sew the wings and back covers *off* the chair, as you would for a loose cover, and then to fit them into place.

(a) Shape your pattern pieces carefully, leaving extra wide turnings. Cut out and tack-stitch the outside and inside wing covers.

(b) Fit the cover very carefully onto the appropriate wing, pulling it down to remove puckers, and half-tack into position.

Alter it if necessary, as it must fit absolutely correctly. Repeat the proceedure with the other wing cover.

(c) Tack-stitch the *outside back edge* of the right wing cover to the *right edge* of the outside back cover, and fit it onto the chair, removing it when you are satisfied.

(d) Tack-stitch the *inside front edge* of the left wing cover to the *left edge* of the inside front cover, and fit it onto the chair, removing it when satisfied.

(e) Machine-stitch the seams so that you have one complete wing cover attached to the inside back cover, and one attached to the outside back cover.

(f) Fit the inside cover first, tacking down at all necessary places, as previously described. Then fit and tack down the outside cover. Stitch seams as necessary.

This is a very useful method for those skilled in dressmaking, but the fitting must be absolutely correct, or the effect will be terrible!

If the tension on the side seams is sufficiently tight, sewing may possibly be omitted, but it is, of course, quite essential along the top.

Loose Cushions

Some chairs are designed to have loose cushions, and some are not, the criterion being that when one sits on a chair, one should be able to rest one's elbows comfortable on the arms of the chair. The addition of a cushion to a chair designed to go through life without one will obviously destroy one's comfort, as does the omission of a cushion which should be there.

Foam Cushions

It is in the making of loose cushions that latex foams and polyesters really come into their own, because they are so easy to use in this instance.

We have previously mentioned the importance of having 'cavity' latex or polyester, that is to say, with horizontal channels running through them. Even the special non-reversible units (you may get one to exactly fit your chair) have 'breathing holes' in the centre.

Having chosen your latex or polyester, decide, before taking the shears to it, whether you want a rounded or squared front

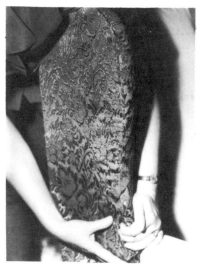

The outside seam of the wing cover is pinned into place.

The pinned wing cover being stretched down to ensure correct fitting.

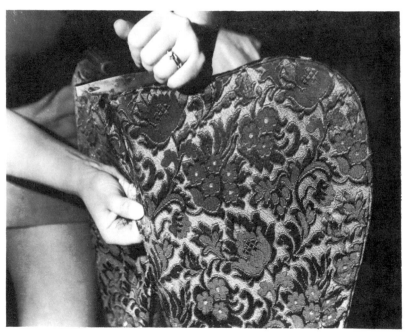

A late adjustment of the tacked cover to ensure a good final fit.

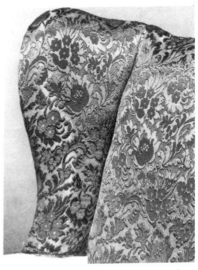

The puckers will disappear when the machined cover is fully stretched.

Re-distribution by means of a regulator will straighten out the crooked seams.

The back cover is half-tacked into position, to be tacked down when the fit is satisfactory.

edge, and whether you would like the centre to be flat or slightly rounded. (Flat cushions are reversible, unless, of course, they are non-reversible units. Centre-rounded cushions are not reversible.) You will normally want two identical foam pieces, stuck together like a sandwich.

Square-Front Flat Cushions

(a) Measure the seat space into which the cushion must fit exactly, and note the measurements. If the shape is other than a plain square, e.g. T-shaped etc, you might do well to cut a pattern from a piece of cardboard.

(b) Mark the measurements on your two pieces of foam, using a felt pen, adding 1 cm. ($\frac{1}{2}$ in.) in every 25 cm. (10 in.) to each measurement, to allow for slight compression.

(c) Cut the foam to size with a pair of sharp shears.

(d) Use the correct adhesive for the type of foam used (your retailer will advise you,) and smear it liberally on both pieces. Most of these glues are inflammable and give off those fumes we are always hearing about. Open windows, turn off gas or electric fires, and don't smoke. And don't inhale the fumes.

(e) When both glued surfaces are tacky, place them together carefully, so that all edges coincide. Leave to dry completely.

(f) Glue a strip of plain strong material, such as 2$\frac{1}{2}$ cm. (1 in.) cotton braid, along the join at the front of the cushion.

Round-Front Flat Cushions

(a) Mark, measure and cut your two foam sheets, as above.

(b) Mark a line in felt pen two inches from what will be the front edge on each foam piece.

(c) Cut from this line diagonally to the front edge of the bottom of the foam sheet, so that the sheet tapers out from top to bottom.

(d) Glue the two pieces together, as above, without gluing the tapered ends, placing the two pieces so that the flat surfaces are outside, and the tapered surfaces in the middle.

(e) When the glue is dry, glue and press the tapered edges together.

The top edge only of a cushion can be rounded by gluing a strip of cotton braid lengthways from the centre front of the

Making Latex foam cushions

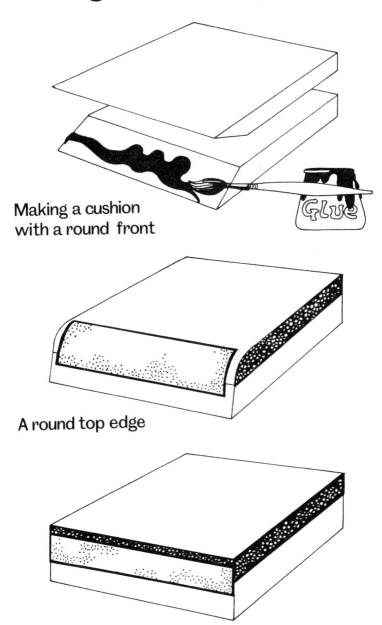

Making a cushion
with a round front

Glue

A round top edge

A square front

cushion well over the top, so that the edge is compressed. Similarly one can round the corners of a cushion with glued cotton braid, as an alternative to cutting off the corner of the foam.

Round-Top Cushions

To round the top of your cushion:

(a) Cut two pieces of foam, and cut a third piece from foam $2\frac{1}{2}$ cm. (1 in.) in depth, three inches smaller all round than the size of your cushion. Mark the size of the smaller piece in the centre of one sheet of foam.

(b) Glue your two cushion pieces, and when you come to place them together, centre the smaller piece on your marked piece of foam, and place the other sheet on top.

Cushion covers are the better for having a zip at the back, so that the cushion can be taken out and aired occasionally.

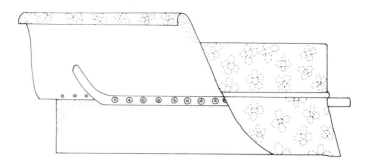

Back tacking a border

Chapter Three

Buttoning, Braiding and other Embellishments

In the previous chapters, we have dealt with what might be called the bare bones of upholstery, describing how to repair and upholster a more or less standard chair in a more or less standard manner.

Now we are going to discuss various ways of embellishing and decorating an armchair by means of buttoning, fluting or piping, and by the addition of braiding and ruching.

Buttoning undoubtedly improves the look of many upholstered chairs, and even if your chair was not previously buttoned, you might like to improve the decorative interest in this fashion.

Buttoning is effected through your cotton cover (if you have one) and upholstery fabric and through your top layer of padding, which is usually wadding. This is done after the fabric has been cut to size (allowing extra fabric as directed in the respective sections) but before it has been fastened down.

The inside back is usually the only part of the chair that is buttoned, although buttoning occasionally extended to the front of the seat. Buttoning tends to make a surface hard, and therefore uncomfortable, and buttoned arms are a source of constant irritation to fidgetty people, who *will* twist the buttons off.

Plain Buttoning

(a) Cut your fabric piece, leaving an extra 2½ cm. (1 in.) on both sides, and at the top and bottom.

(b) Decide where the buttons should go, measure out and mark the sites on the fabric, using chalk or crossed pins. When

Buttoning a Cushion

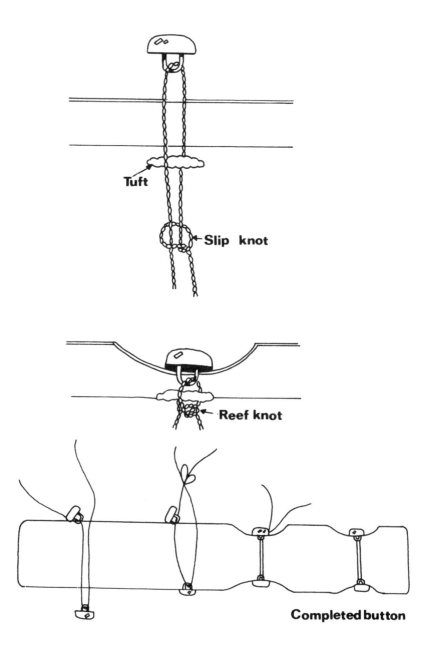

Tuft

Slip knot

Reef knot

Completed button

all sites are marked satisfactorily snip a tiny hole in each site, just big enough to take the shank of the button.

(c) Thread a length of twine through the button shank, and pass *both* ends through the eye of a straight upholstery needle.

(d) Stitch through fabric and padding and out through the chair back, and join twine ends in a slip knot.

(e) Take a small strip of stout cotton material or felt, and insert it between the padding and the slip knot.

(f) Pull the slip knot as tight as possible, and tie the ends of the twine in a reef knot.

Note It is essential that the tightness of the twine should be the same on all buttons, or the buttoning will be uneven. This can be a hazard for beginners, and a certain amount of care must be taken. In time, the process becomes automatic. Make sure that you are completely satisfied with each buttoning before fastening the fabric onto the chair.

A small ring of latex foam placed under the upholstery fabric, with a tiny hole for the button shank to pass through, will deepen the buttoning effect, but this does not constitute deep buttoning.

Deep Buttoning

Deep buttoning, in which the fabric is actually pleated by the buttons, was very popular in Victorian times, and is now back in fashion. The process is a little more elaborate than plain buttoning, but well worth the extra trouble.

Using Hair or Fibre

(a) Mark out button sites in a diamond pattern on the *top layer of your padding*, using large crossed pins.

(b) Mark the sites on the fabric, with an extra 4 cm. (1½ in.) between each button site. (It is as well to do this before you cut your fabric to size, because the amount of extra fabric will depend on the number of buttons you decide to have, and you may not want to decide on this without a little experimentation.) You will find it a help to mark complete diagonal lines, with pins on your padding, with chalk on your fabric, to help you work out the correct button sites. Remove the pins from the padding, except those actually marking the sites, when those sites have been established. The centre button site in padding and fabric must coincide. As you establish the other button sites, remove the unwanted pins.

(c) Secure your centre button site without tying off the twine ends, and stuff around it with a handful of hair or fibre covered with wadding. Use just enough padding to bring the next button site to coincide with the marked site on the padding below. This must be done with some expertise, because too little will leave an unsightly dip, and too much will prevent the next button sites on fabric and padding from coinciding. Secure this next button, and pad around it as for the first button. Make sure that you are satisfied with each 'pocket' before proceeding. Tie off the ends of twine when satisfied.

(d) The pulling tight of the twine for tying off will cause pleats to form, and these look best if you arrange them so that each button is at the centre of four major pleats, each going out in 'rays' with the button in the centre. Where possible, they should run parallel to other button pleats, as this improves the appearance of the whole surface considerably. The direction and smoothness of the pleats should be attended to as you work on each button, as very little can be done with them after the job is completed. A regulator will help you to get the pleats in position.

Using Polyester and Latex Foam

(a) Using a thick layer of foam, or two layers together, mark out the sites with a felt pen, preferably drawing diagonal lines first.

(b) Snip holes on the sites for the button shanks. If using two thin sheets, snip through both of them.

(c) Start with the centre site, and work as for plain buttoning, pulling the twine really tight.

(d) Arrange pleats as described above.

Note It is obviously easier to effect deep buttoning with polyesters or latex, but you get far better final results when using natural fibres.

Fluting

Fluting was often used in Victorian chairs, and resembles

deep pleating running vertically down the back of the chair, the flutes narrowing towards the bottom. It lends decorative interest to a large-backed and otherwise rather dull chair, and is extremely useful when you are using narrow material, as fluting always has an 'intentional' look.

There are no rules regarding the distance between flutes, but they are usually about 10–13 cm. (4–5 in.) wide at the top, tapering slightly towards the base. Very narrow flutes have a rather fussy appearance.

There are two methods of fluting, one of which is illustrated, the other described below. The cutting out of flutes really is a point of no return, and it is often a wise move to pin your material along the proposed flute lines, and drape it across the chair to see if you like the effect. This also helps you to decide the distance between the flutes. The chair may well remain in your home for a generation, and it is as well to be perfectly pleased with every improvement you make to it.

As with buttoning, your fabric is fluted before it is fastened down to the inside back of the chair. In this case, you will need a strong backing fabric, such as hessian or stout cotton. For this reason, there is no need to apply cotton covering over your padding, unless you feel personally that this will make your work easier.

(a) Your backing fabric will only need to stretch from the top of the chair to about 5 cm. (2 in.) below the top of the seat, but your upholstery fabric, of course, must continue on to be fastened below the bottom rail, as inside back covers usually do. Remember this when you are marking out your flutes. If the flutes are to be cut (see below), the tapered base of them will go just below the line of the top of the seat, and you will sew on an extra piece to go down to the bottom rail, making sure that the seam is hidden below the top of the seat.

(b) Mark the lines of the flutes on your backing fabric, using chalk or felt pen, or lines of pins. The bottom of the flutes will come about 4–5 cm. (1–2 in.) below the bottom line of the inside back.

(c) Mark out the flutes on your upholstery fabric, making the spaces between them a little larger than on the backing fabric. The extra amount will depend on how deep you want your seams to be recessed. The fabric must bulge enough to make a series of identical conical pockets.

(d) If you are having straight flutes (properly called 'channels'), or if your flutes are only very slightly tapered, you can simply pin the flute lines on your two layers of fabric, and seam along the lines. If your tapering is sharp, you will find it easier to cut them out of your two layers of fabric, leaving an extra centimetre ($\frac{1}{2}$ in.) on each side for the seam, and sew them together. A preliminary pinning will show you if this is advisable, as a large piece of fan-shaped material is not always easy to deal with, and it may be difficult to get the flutes even, especially towards the bottom.

(e) Sew across the bottom of your flutes.

(f) Fill your flutes with padding material. It is possible to buy cotton fluting material in a long roll, or you can use foam chips, or ordinary natural fibre wrapped in wadding. Push the padding down with a stick. A piece of dowel is quite adequate, although special 'stuffing sticks' are available. Make sure that each flute is evenly filled, not only along its own length and breadth, but in relation to other flutes.

(g) If you have cut your flutes, sew on the extra piece of fabric needed to stretch from the seat edge to the bottom of the rail.

(h) Half-tack your fluted piece to the top and bottom frames of the chair (as you would for an ordinary inside back cover) placing one tack in each seam. Make sure that the flutes are placed absolutely accurately, especially from top to bottom, as crooked flutes are very noticeable. Measure if necessary. Stretch the fabric well between flutes while tacking. If you have filled the flutes sufficiently, the joining seams will be recessed, and therefore invisible.

(i) When completely satisfied, tack the fabric over the back of the top framework rail (where it will be covered by the outside back cover), under the bottom rail, and at the sides.

Note The very best 'dummy run' for this exercise would be a fluted cushion, in which case the flutes look best if they meet at a point on the centre of the bottom front edge. The filling of the actual cushion should be kept fairly flat for best effect. Fluted cushions, if not particularly to your own taste in decor, answer

Wadding is laid on the inside back of the chair, and tucked well into the flutes.

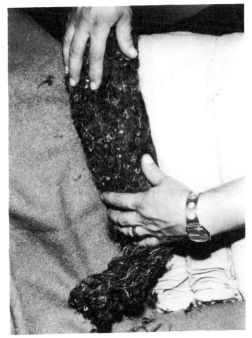

Extra padding is laid along each flute to deepen the effect.

The fabric is not wide enough to cover the whole of the inside back in one width, which is done in three sections. To machine the pieces together before placing them could create a problem of seams not coinciding with recesses. Note that the flutes on the right have been recessed by hand, those on the left have not.

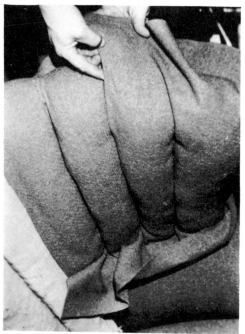

The fabric is laid into place, half-tacked over the back, and beneath the bottom rail. It is then pleated by hand.

The fabric is pressed
into the recesses with
the edge of the hand
and kept there with
upholstery skewers.

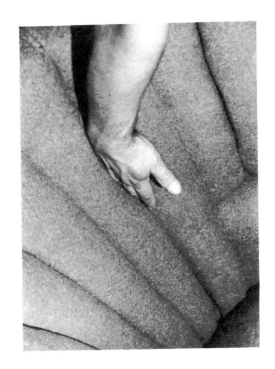

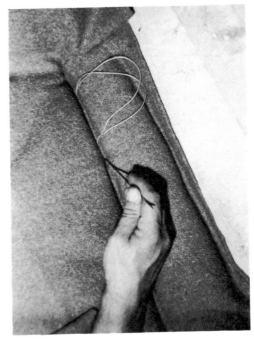

A seam is stitched
down the recesses,
each stitch going
right through to the
back of the chair. A
long   upholstery
needle and uphol-
stery   thread   is
needed.

When the seam is finished, the thread is looped around a tack in the top framework, the tack then being hammered home.

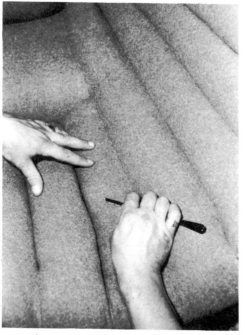

A regulator is used to even out the padding. This finishing touch gives a professional look to your work.

many a Christmas gift problem.

Channelling

The technique of channelling is identical with that of fluting, except that channels are rectangular, and flutes tapered. While channels are only used on square-backed chairs, they have an application in the modern chaise-longue or day-bed, when the channels usually run across the width, and not down the length.

Piping

Many armchairs have piped seams, in which a length of fabric-covered cord is incorporated between two fabric edges where they join. Sometimes all seams are piped, and sometimes piping is restricted to, say, the front edge of the seat and the front and top of the arms. This is purely a matter of personal choice, and it is by no means necessary to follow the method previously used on any particular chair.

Piping is often made from the actual upholstery material used to cover a chair (extra fabric being needed in this case) but a contrasting piping looks well against a plain fabric, as does a plain piping against a patterned fabric if it picks out one of the predominating colours. Piping made from patterned or striped fabrics often has an unattractive 'bitty' look, and it is usually better to substitute one made from plain fabric.

Very thick fabrics, and those with a high nap, such as plush or velvet, do not usually make successful piping.

Preparation of Piping

There are a number of cords suitable for piping, including special piping cord, but nylon cord bought at any hardware shop is quite suitable. The stoutness of the cord depends on your material, since obviously a tweed will need a thicker cord than a satin or chintz. A quick run over the chair seams with a tape-measure should tell you how much cord you need, and it is better to have it all in one piece. If you do have to join cord, fray the ends, overlap them, and bind them with thread, sewing it through and through before finishing off. The joined ends should match the rest of the cord in thickness and roundness.

The material to cover the cord should be cut on the bias in

strips about 5 cm. (2 in.) wide. When the strips are joined, they should lie in an absolutely straight line. You may need several yards of piping, and it is better to get it all done in one operation.

To sew piping on a machine, you will need a piping or zipper foot, and if you have neither, you may well be better off enduring the tedium of sewing by hand, unless you are really expert at machine sewing, because the seam must be really close to the cord, and yet not run into it.

Lay your cord in the centre of the *back* of the fabric strip, and fold the two edges of the strip together. Seam as close to the cord as possible without sewing into it, making sure that the cord is tightly covered.

How to Place Piping

We will take as example the laying of piping along the top of a chair back. The same technique is applied wherever piping is laid.

The piping will look best at the front edge of the top of the chair, and since piping is laid at the join between two seams, the inside back cover will stop at the front edge of the top rail, and not be continued beyond it, as it would be if we were not laying piping.

If the top frame of the chair is rather wide, you may consider that it would look better if you piped both edges, i.e. both the front and back of the top rail. In this case both inside and outside back covers would stop short at the outside edges of the rail, and a strip of fabric would be cut to cover the rail itself, the two long seams of which would be piped.

However, to lay piping on the inside edge only, proceed as follows:

(a) When fastening your inside back cover, make sure that the turned-in edge coincides with the *inside* top edge of the framework rail. It should be back-tacked for a neater finish.

(b) Place your piping so that the seam of the covered cord is flush with the top edge of the inside back cover, and the double edge of the piping fabric lying on the uncovered top rail.

(c) Tack through the double thickness of piping fabric close to the seam, placing tacks about 5 cm (2 in.) apart, and stretching reasonably tight between tacks. The cord of the piping should rise a little as the tacks are placed. Check between each tack that the piping is positioned correctly, as nothing looks worse than bad piping.

(d) Take your outside back cover and turn the top edge under. Cut a thin strip of cardboard about 1 cm. ($\frac{1}{2}$ in.) wide, and as long as the width of the cover and slip it under the turned-over edge. Pin it if necessary.

(e) Place it over the double thickness of piping fabric lying on the top rail, and push it against the piped cord. Half-tack it into position, using three tacks only (one at each end, one in the middle) and stretching it well between tacks.

(f) Test that the rest of the outside back cover falls into place correctly, especially if you are using striped or patterned fabric, where the slightest crookedness will be very noticeable. Check, too, that the outside edges and the bottom of the cover reach the uprights to which they must be attached.

(g) When you are satisfied with the fall of the outside back cover, and with the way your edges lie on each side of the piping, stitch the top edge of your outside back cover to the seam of the piping (not to the seam itself) and then remove the three tacks.

If you have become an expert at back-tacking, and prefer it to stitching a seam by hand, you can back-tack the top edge of the outside back cover onto the top rail, but it must be positioned correctly, hard against your piping cord. You must also be perfectly sure that your cover will hang down the back correctly. Back-tacking is extremely tedious to remove.

Front Arm Facings

If you intend to pipe around a front arm facing, this should be done after the turned-in facing has been hemmed, the two thicknesses of the piping being laid behind the facing edge so that the piping seam and the edge of the facing coincide. The piping is then sewn into position.

Note Many upholstery books, especially those of American origin, refer to piping as 'cording', but since the word 'cording' is usually taken to denote the tying of springs in a chair seat, the word 'piping' is preferable, and indeed, more familiar.

The practice of covering seams with uncovered silk cord is

not recommended, and is seldom used, as such cord is short-lived, and tends to come unstitched with use.

Braiding

Braiding is known in the trade as 'gimp', and is normally used to give a finished effect between a fabric edge and a show-wood framework piece where back-tacking has not been effected, and there is a visible tack line. It also helps to keep flat the turned-in edge of a thick fabric.

Braid is available in a wide variety of colours, and you can be reasonably certain of obtaining a good match or interesting contrast.

Ruche

Ruche can be considered a more elaborate type of braid, and comes in three varieties:

(1) Loop ruche, in which the threads of the pile are not cut.
(2) Cut ruche, in which the threads are cut.
(3) Rope ruche, which, as the name implies, is in the form of a rope.

Ruche performs the same function, and is attached in the same way as braid, being stitched into place. The use of tacks to fasten braid or ruching defeats its object, which is to cover a tack-line in the first place.

It is also possible to buy silk fringing for the same purpose, but although it was extremely popular in Victorian times, it is now somewhat out of place, unless you are reupholstering a Victorian piece in strict period context. It looks well on velvet-covered ottomans or footstools, but the appearance of too much embellishment on an armchair or sofa is something of which one can quickly become tired.

Chapter Four

Sofas, Stools and Box Ottomans

Once you have reupholstered an armchair, you have completed just about all the basic techniques, and should be able to tackle almost any upholstery job, taking any slight variations in your stride. Obviously no book on upholstery can instruct you, in minute detail, how to deal with every possible permutation and combination in padded furniture, but once you have completed one armchair, you will find yourself adapting your knowledge to suit any similar project.

Your mind retains the knowledge gained from any chair you strip down, and the decision to reupholster in exactly the same way, or to use a different technique, is guided by that knowledge, by your own personal taste, or by a spirit of experimentation.

But an armchair is not the only piece of furniture that requires reupholstering, and in this chapter we deal with box ottomans, dining chairs, stools, footstools and sofas.

Sofas and Chaises Longues

A sofa can be regarded as little more than an overgrown armchair, with extra spaces between the arms. Chaises longues and love-seats similarly resemble extenuated chairs, and if you can deal with the chair, you will have no problems with the larger pieces.

Sofas, chaises longues and love-seats sometimes have recessed seats, in which the webbing stretches from side to side *beneath* the framework rails, rather than from the top of them. This slight difference does not alter the methods of springing or padding, but usually necessitates a good hard edge on all parts not protected by the back, to avoid the rim of the framework being felt through the padding. A hard edge is better in this case than a fibre roll or rubber profile. It should be well covered with wadding, and the final cover carefully fitted down reasonably tightly to give a smooth appearance.

Box Ottomans

Ottomans can be made from a solid box, or on a frame, and are normally about 38 cm. (15 in.) high, so that they can be comfortably used as seats.

If you are using a frame (which can be bought at handicraft shops or made at home) cover the four sides, inside and out, with cardboard or hessian. If you are starting with a ready-made box (e.g. an old ottoman), remove the base and lid, so that you are left with the four sides. Also remove hinges, lid strap, old upholstery, padding and lining.

Lining

(1) *Sides*

(a) Using a cotton material, or possibly a sateen to blend with your outside covering fabric, cut four pieces to line the sides, adding 5 cm. (2 in.) to all measurements.

(b) Turn the edges under, line the longest sides first by tacking the lining to the bottom, and straining it up to the top, tacking it about 2 cm. ($\frac{3}{4}$ in.) below the top edge. Back-tacking can be used along the lower edges.

(c) Take the side edges of the fabric round the corner of the adjacent side, and tack into position. (These tacks will be covered when the shorter sides are lined.) Do this with both ends of both pieces of fabric, and you have your two long sides properly lined.

(d) Line the two short sides, tacking top and bottom, with the side edges fitting flush into the box corner right the way down, instead of being carried round the adjacent side. One is often instructed at this point to slip stitch down this corner seam, but this is a bit difficult to get at. If you have stretched your fabric tight enough from top to bottom, the folded edge should stay in place.

(2) Base

Even if you are using a frame, you will need a plywood base, and if you have bought a 'kit', you should find it included. It is covered before being fitted into place.

Line the base by straining the cloth evenly over all four edges, and tacking it around the very edge. Screw the base onto the bottom of the frame or box, and the tack heads will be hidden. If your lining is lumpy, or your tack heads crooked, the base will not screw on properly, and the result will be unsatisfactory.

Alternative Method
The base can also be lined in the following way:

(a) Cut a piece of stout cardboard accurately to the *inside* dimensions of the box, less $\frac{1}{2}$ cm. ($\frac{1}{4}$ in.) on all sides.

(b) Cover one side of it, carrying the fabric over to the back on all sides to a depth of one inch. Mitre corners neatly. Glue the 'carry over' at the back.

(c) When the glue is completely dry, force the cardboard down to the bottom of the box, where, if it is a good fit, it should remain in position. A little glue will add to the permanency.

The box lid is normally lined in the same fashion, after the rest of the upholstery is complete.

External Upholstery
The decision to pad or not to pad the sides is yours entirely, and this largely depends on the fabric used, and the type of furniture with which the box must blend. Certainly unpadded ottomans have a rather meagre look, and a certain amount of padding rounds out the corners and prolongs the life of your fabric. The top, of course, will have to be padded in any case, as it is designed to be used as a seat.

Almost any type of padding can be used (polyesters do well here) and there are no problems in technique, as long as you remember to pad round the corners, and to avoid *absolutely* padding on the top of the frame of the box itself, and on the base of the lid, or the lid won't close properly.

Before cutting your fabric, consider the fact that you are going to have at least *one* vertical seam somewhere on the outside of the ottoman, and decide where you would prefer it to be. Your technique can vary between the cutting of one continuous piece of fabric, wrapping it round the four sides of the box, and having one vertical seam, or cutting four pieces, one for each side, and having a seam at each corner. Possibly the most reliable method is to cut one piece which will go round the front and two sides to reach the back corners, and one to cover the back, so that you have two vertical seams at the two back corners. It is a curious fact that two seams in matching positions are less conspicious than one odd seam, the two seams being balanced off by correct positioning. In any event, proceed as follows:

(a) Back-tack your cover (edges turned under) to the *top inside edge of the box*, so that the tacks securing the lining in place are covered. Make quite sure that the edge of your cardboard strip does not come above the level of your box top edge.

(b) Pull the fabric down outside the box, and turn the box over to half-tack the fabric to the base, making the correct V-cuts to achieve neat cornering. The fabric must be really tight before you hammer home the tacks.

(c) On the site of your seam (or seams) carry the edge of one piece round the corner, and turn in the edges of the other so that it coincides all the way down with the actual corner. Pin it into position, adjusting until you are completely satisfied with the set of the fabric in all directions. Then slip-stitch the seam.

Alternative Method

You can fit and tack your cover, and then remove it for seaming, fitting it into position on completion. You cannot, of course, back-tack when using this method, and the top edge is usually fastened to the top inside edge of the box with gimp pins, and then braided. This method does not usually give such a good finish, but is far quicker.

Upholstering the Lid

Padded Lid

If you are using a frame, make a webbing base, and cover it with hessian before padding. If the box has a wooden lid, this can be used as a base, but it must be well padded, or it will be uncomfortable. There must be no padding under the frame, as it prevents the box from closing. A hessian or cotton cover should be applied under the upholstery fabric.

Spring Top Lid

If your box has a wooden top, you might like to try this method of springing, to make a more comfortable seat.

(a) Cover the top of the lid with felt, to stop the springs from rattling. It can be glued at the edges to keep it in position.

(b) Take four 10 cm. (4 in.) 9 gauge springs, and place them well away from the edge, and equidistant without the bases touching.

(c) Cut 12 pieces of webbing each about $7\frac{1}{2}$ cm. (3 in.) long.

(d) Take one of these pieces and folding in the cut edges, tack one turned-in edge on one side of the bottom coil of the spring, and the other on the other side, so that the bottom coil is held down by the tacked-down webbing 'tag'. Use three such tags to each spring, and fasten down all four springs in this fashion.

(e) Cord the springs as instructed on page 17.

(f) Cover the springs with hessian, and tack it to the outside edges of the box lid all round, making sure that it is strained tight.

(g) Sew spring tops to hessian.

(h) Bridle-stitch around the edge, and several times across the top, leaving your stitching to hang in 10 cm. (4 in) loops.

(i) Cover the top with fibre, well teased out, pushing it through the loops. Cover with a layer of wadding after you have the whole seat well padded.

(j) Cover with cotton fabric, bridle stitch around the edge, and tack down all round to the *underside* of the lid.

(g) Apply your upholstery cover.

Whether you decide to pad or spring your ottoman top, there are two ways of fitting the cover if the lid is deep. You can either 'throw' your fabric over, pull it down and finish the corners by mitring, or you can cover the top and sides separately. The latter, of course, creates a seam right down the lid just below the top, which lends itself to piping or braiding but set against this is the fact that you must be sure to get a neat mitre on what may be a very deep corner.

The cover is tacked to the underside of the lid, and this is best effected by placing one temporary tack in the centre of each side edge first, to ensure that you get the cover correctly positioned. The fabric must be very smooth and the tacks driven home properly when the job is finished, or the lid will not close properly. Make sure, too, that the fabric does not impede the movement of the hinges.

Lining the Lid

Line the lid according to directions for lining the base, including the gluing of the material turn-over on the underside of a correctly cut piece of cardboard, and then by gluing this on the underside of the lid. A few temporary tacks will keep it in place while the glue dries.

Finishing

(a) Choose hinges appropriate to the size and weight of the box, and fix them to the lid and back of the box. Recess them if necessary, and make sure that they are invisible from the outside when the box is closed. If you are reupholstering an old ottoman, the decision regarding recessing may already have been taken for you.

(b) Construct two 'straps' of fabric, fixing each from opposite insides of the box lid into the inside of the box itself, to prevent the lid from falling too far back. The straps should allow the lid to fall further than the vertical position, or the lid may close by reason of its own weight, possibly capturing your hand in the process. Sections of brass chain can be substituted for the fabric straps.

(c) Fit castors or silent domes to the base of the box. Ottomans are usually too heavy to lift, and dragging can damage carpets.

Note Ottoman tops lend themselves to deep buttoning, and if you intend to use this technique, holes must be drilled through the wooden lid (if there is one), so that the button twine can pass through. These holes, of course, must coincide with your button sites above, and you should note the distance between your drilled holes, so that you can find them easily by prodding with your needle. Plain buttoning can be effected through the padding only, but you can get splendid deep buttoning if your twine comes right through the lid and is pulled really tight. The twine ends are tacked down to the underside of the lid.

Stools and Footstools

Stools vary greatly in design, from fat squat box-like ones, to those with high legs and usually hard uncomfortable seats.

Having reached this stage in upholstery techniques, there is little that can be added with regard to stools, they being padded or sprung according to type. Often the webbing is recessed, i.e. attached to the base of the frame, often in conjunction with a show-wood frame. In this case, the seat should be padded to be flat, while in stools without show-wood frames, a rounded centre seat is more comfortable, and looks better.

Many stools have recessed legs, i.e. instead of being flush with the seat corners, the legs are attached to the *inside* of the seat framework. These are easier to deal with, because your fabric can be brought under the framework and tacked there. But where the legs are actually at the corner, you will have to deal with it as shown on page 98.

Or you can snip the fabric so that a piece goes on each side of the leg, and the centre piece is folded under and lies against the front surface of the leg. If your fabric is stretched tight enough, this portion will not need to be tacked down.

Stools with deep seats without show-wood frames can be upholstered in the same way as box ottomans, i.e. either in one piece with mitred corners, or with separate top and side pieces.

Dining-Room Chairs

These either have a loose seat which drops into the frame, or a fully upholstered seat, either padded or sprung.

Loose Seats

Although the term 'loose seat' is used, it should be large enough to fit tightly into the framework of the chair. If your

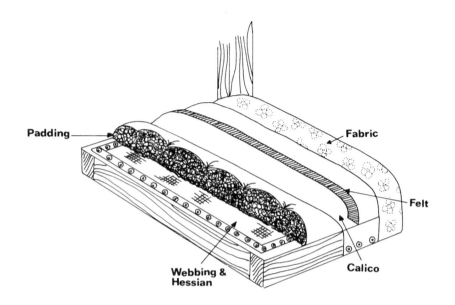

Padding

Fabric

Felt

Calico

Webbing & Hessian

Fitting a cover on a square corner

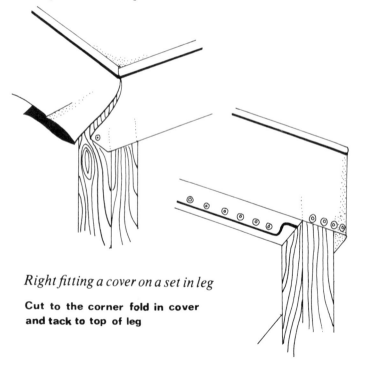

Right fitting a cover on a set in leg

Cut to the corner fold in cover and tack to top of leg

chair seat 'works loose' with the passing of time, and the structure is in all respects sound, the treatment is no more drastic than the tacking of strips of cardboard along the inside of the chair frame, making sure that the cardboard does not show above the frame edge when the seat is in position.

If you reupholster a dining-room chair seat, you should take care that no padding carries over the outside of the frame, and that your fabric is smooth in all places, especially at the corners (pleat or mitre for neat corners), or the seat will not fit into the frame. Snip away excess fabric at the corners if necessary.

Should your dining-room chair have a plywood seat, you will find it much more comfortable if you substitute webbing. Our Victorian ancestors, although they took their food very seriously, did not consider comfort an aid to digestion.

Cover the webbing with hessian tacked to the outer edge of the seat frame, and sew bridle-stitch loops, through which the padding can be stuffed. The loops keep the padding in position, as you can't use a fibre roll or hard edge in this case. If you apply a cotton cover over the padding, don't turn the edges in, to avoid extra bulkiness at the outer edges. Take it to the outsides of the frame, and trim it level with the bottom line. Apply your fabric cover in the same way, and tack a strip of narrow cotton tape along the bottom edge of the fabric to prevent it from fraying, using as few tacks as you need to keep it in place. If your upholstery fabric is thinner than ordinary household tape, turn in the edges and omit the tape.

Fixed Seat

These, of course, have no show-wood frames, and can be sprung and padded, or more usually simply padded. If you should decide to spring the seat of a dining-room chair, the springing is limited to five springs, one at each corner and one in the middle, the springs touching neither the outside edge nor each other. Hard edges are usually sewn, and the seat slightly domed in the centre.

Dining-chair backs have upright rails, and when fitting first your cotton cover and then your upholstery fabric, you will have to make use of the techniques described on page 59.

Fitting Your Cover

Once again, the techniques have already been described, and the most applicable instructions are those given for the upholstering of an ottoman lid. Again, the depth of the seat will dictate whether you should cut your cover in one piece, or with separate pieces for the sides. Where the latter is decided upon, two seams, one above the back of each back leg, are most usual.

It is very rare to find a dining-room chair with an upholstered seat and show-wood frame, but should yours conform to this design, it is best to finish your fabric edge with braiding, since you can only back-tack one edge of it. As an alternative to braid, a continuous line of brass or bronze headed tacks at the very edge of the fabric looks well on a dining-room chair, especially if you have a plain, solid colour cover. The tacking must be very straight and even, or the effect is spoilt.

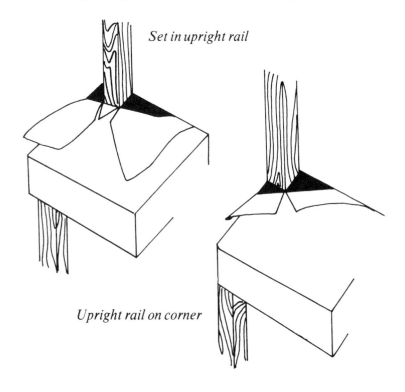

Set in upright rail

Upright rail on corner

Chapter Five

Loose Covers

It is possible to buy stretch loose covers for armchairs and sofas, but it often appears that one of the requirements is that they should not fit properly, which only goes to prove that arm-chairs and sofas are highly individual pieces of furniture, and one seems almost bound to own an 'odd man out'.

A chair with a good loose cover will remain in perfect condition for ten, twenty or even fifty years . . . certainly until the children grow up. Loose covers, even though they can look as attractive as actual upholstery, if they are properly made, are considered by some people to be a rather cheese-paring economy. But a generation ago, they were considered plain common sense, and many people had two sets, one for winter and one for summer, the latter being made of material lighter in colour and texture.

There were interesting social sidelights to loose covers in those days, the wealthy who closed their country houses in winter and their town houses in summer, usually had loose covers made from brown holland (now exclusively a fabric for making window blinds) to protect their upholstered furniture left in a closed house, this obviously providing better protection than dust-sheets. Less well-endowed people made loose covers out of strong washable material such as cretonne, which kept its colour through many launderings, (with vinegar and salt to prevent fading) while people who had to be especially careful with their furniture, who kept the 'parlour' for special occasions, often had *two* sets of covers, one on top of the other. The top one was made of cotton or holland, and the under one of chintz or other patterned material. It was a matter of social nicety which cover confronted a guest, since an ordinary visitor would sit on cotton loose covers, and a more important one the patterned loose covers (the top layer having been whisked away in an instant), and the actual upholstery being shown to view as a mark of the very greatest respect, possibly only at weddings and funerals.

This may raise a smile when we read about it today, but loose covers, in single or multiple layers, are the reason that much original antique upholstery remains in good condition today. In addition to their protective qualities, loose covers can be removed for laundering.

Outside of the fact that you will be dealing with large bulky pieces of material, with your sewn piece getting larger and bulkier as you work, there is nothing difficult in making a loose cover, although the word 'loose' must not be taken to mean 'baggy'. The tighter a cover fits, the better it will look, and the best test of it is that it should not be immediately identifiable as a loose cover, but should fit as closely as the upholstery underneath.

There is a good range of suitable materials available these days, including denim, which makes an excellent material for loose covers, and various 'stretch' fabrics including jersey, which looks particularly well, although it is not renowned for its wearing quality.

We have already dealt previously with the drafting of a pattern, and the proceedure is the same here, except for the fact that in addition to half-inch turnings on all seams, you must leave 13 cm. (5 in.) 'tuck-ins' at the bottom of inside back, and at the back and on both sides of the seat cover. You will also need to have a 13 cm. (5 in.) hem at the bottom of the inside back and inside arms, the extra weight of which will help to keep the cover from riding up.

You will also find it easier if the cover at the front of the seat comes down to the level of the bottom of the front arm facings. This protects a show-wood front, if you have one, enables the cover to fit better, and gives the whole job a more finished look.

Your loose cushion, if you have one, should have a zip fastener or hooks and eyes on one side, so that the cover can be washed. You will also need a placket at the side of one of the front legs (where it is least visible), with a zip or hooks and eyes, to make it easier to remove and replace the cover.

To be more specific.

Start by cutting your series of rectangles as follows:

(a) *Inside Back* Measure along a centre line from top to bottom, allowing an extra 15 cm. (6 in.), 2½ cm. (1 in.) for the turning at the top, and 12½ cm. (5 in.) for the tuck-in into the back of the seat. Measure a line from side to side across the width at the widest point, adding 5 cm. (2 in.) for turnings, one at each side.

(b) *Seat Cover* Measure across the centre of the seat from front to back, adding 15 cm. (6 in.), 2½ cm. (1 in.) for the front turning, and 12½ cm. (5 in.) for the tuck-in at the back. Measure through the centre from side to side, adding 25 cm (10 in.), 12½ cm. (5 in.) for a tuck-in at either side.

(c) *Seat Front* Measure from side to side, adding 5 cm. (2 in.) for turnings. Measure the depth to a point level with the bottom of the arm facings, and *then add* 15 cm. (6 in.), 2½ cm. (1 in.), one for the top turnings, and 12½ cm. (5 in.) for the deep hem at the bottom. This gives extra weight to keep the cover in position.

(d) *Inside Arm*

Scroll Arm Even if your actual upholstery is pleated over the front of the arm, you will find it much easier if you only bring your loose cover up to the edge of the front of the arm, and make a full-front facing, so that pleating of this part of the cover is avoided. This seam, which comes at the exact edge of the front of the arm, looks well piped, as do most seams on a loose cover.

Measure from the point over the bolster of the arm down to the bottom of the inside arm where it meets the seat. Add 15 cm. (6 in.), 2½ cm. (1 in.) for the turning, 12½ cm. (5 in.) for the tuck-in. Measure from the back to the front, taking the measurement from the *outside* of the arm, and not from the join of the inner arm and back. Add 5 cm. (2 in.) for turnings. Make a pattern for the other inner arm.

Straight Arm Simply follow the design of the piece on which you are working, remembering to leave an extra 2½ cm. (1 in.) for all turnings, and the 12½ cm. (5 in.) tuck-in at the bottom.

(e) *Front Arm Facing*

Curved Arms Measure from the highest part of the curve to the bottom, adding 15 cm. (6 in.), 2½ cm. (1 in.) for the turning, and

$12\frac{1}{2}$ cm. (5 in.) for the deep hem. Measure the greatest width, and add 5 cm. (2 in.) for turnings.

(f) *Outside Back* Measure along a centre line from the top (or from the highest point) to the bottom, adding 15 cm. (6 ins.), $2\frac{1}{2}$ cm. (1 in.) for turnings, and $12\frac{1}{2}$ cm. (5 in.) for the deep hem. Measure across the widest width, adding 5 cm. (2 in.) for turnings.

(g) *Outside Arms* Measure from the location of your top arm seam to the bottom of the bottom rail, adding 15 cm. (6 in.), $2\frac{1}{2}$ cm (1 in.) for the turning, and $12\frac{1}{2}$ cm. (5 in.) for the deep hem. Measure across from the location of the front seam to the point where the end of the arm meets the outside back cover, i.e. at the back of the back upright rail. Allow 5 cm. (2 in.) for turnings.

Cut your rectangles, and shape each pattern piece as you did when applying new upholstery, making sure that you have your deep hems and tuck-ins in the right place, and leaving $2\frac{1}{2}$ cm. turnings where necessary.

Obviously you will need a little more material for a loose cover, because of the deep hems and tuck-ins, but if you lay out your pattern as you did when measuring your upholstery fabric, once again you will get an accurate idea of the amount required. If you intend to pipe your seams using the same fabric, you will need *at least* another 45 cm. (18 in.) and don't forget to include the pattern for your loose cushion, if you have one, in your layout.

Sewing Up
(Pin and tack-stitch all pieces first.)

(a) Tack-stitch the *bottom* of the *inside back* cover to the *back* of the seat cover. (Don't worry if it looks immense. You have two $12\frac{1}{2}$ cm. (5 in.) tuck-ins which will disappear behind the seat.)

(b) Tack-stitch the *bottoms* of your two *inside arm* covers to the *sides* of the *seat cover*. (Again the massive tuck-ins.) Make sure that you get the fronts of the cover to the front, and the backs to the back. This is not flippancy, but a warning regarding a very common mistake in making loose covers.

(c) Tack-stitch the back edge of the *inside arm* to the bottom of the inside back, from the point at which the inside back meets the top of the arm. It is essential that this should fit perfectly, because we are coming to the point where the work will become conspicuous.

Thus you have tack-stitched the cover for the inside of the chair.

Turning the cover inside out, fit it on the chair, and make sure that all pieces are in their correct positions.

(a) Take the *front seat piece*, and place it with the back towards you, so that the centre of the top edge coincides *exactly* with the centre of the front of the seat. (Measure it out.) Working from this point, pin the *top edge* of it to the *bottom of the seat cover*.

(b) Pin the *front arm facings* (also inside out) to the *front edges* of the *inside and outside arm covers*. Pin the sides of the *front seat* to the *bottom inside* of the front arm facings.

(c) Pin the *outside back* to the *inside back* right around until it meets the top of the arms on each side. Then pin the lower part of the *outside back* to the outer edge of the *outside arm cover*, the front of which is pinned to the edge of the arm facing.

Remove the cover, and tack-stitch seams, removing pins. Leave about eight inches at the base of the join between the front of the inside arm cover and the front arm facing unstitched for the placket. Fit again, and make any necessary adjustments. Machine-stitch all seams including the deep hem.

To sew the placket, face both seams with a strip of fabric. Sew hooks along one side and eyes along the other, or fit in a zip fastener.

Finishing

The appearance of the cover will be improved if you cut away the deep hem on the corners of the legs, where it sometimes looks a little bunchy. This is done by a V-cut at the corner, the raw edges being bound with bias tape to prevent fraying. Tapes are sometimes sewn at the corners to be tied around the legs, and this prevents the cover from riding up.

Where chair legs slope inwards, the cover will need to be

tapered at the bottom, but you should be able to spot this when you fit your cover on inside out.

Note. If you have cut your pattern for 2½ cm. (1 in.) turnings, then 2½ cm. (1 in.) turnings you must *take*, or your cover will be too big. If you have a really non-fraying material, you can use smaller turnings, especially if you are prepared to bind the raw edges with bias, but as a general practice it is better to take large turnings, and trim the edges afterwards if necessary, because large turnings give you that much leeway if you cut a little too 'close to the bone'.